THE
PSI MIND
IN ACTION

THE PSI MIND IN ACTION

Exploring the Powers of
the Human Mind beyond
the Brain

ROBERT A. CHARMAN

www.whitecrowbooks.com

The PSI Mind in Action

Copyright © 2023 by Robert A. Charman. All rights reserved.

Published by White Crow Books, an imprint
of White Crow Productions Ltd.

The right of Robert A. Charman to be identified as the
author of this work has been asserted by him in accordance
with the Copyright, Design and Patents act 1988.

No part of this book may be reproduced, copied or used in any
form or manner whatsoever without written permission, except
in the case of brief quotations in reviews and critical articles.

A CIP catalogue record for this book is available from the British Library.

For information, contact White Crow Books by
e-mail: info@whitecrowbooks.com.

Cover Design by Astrid@Astridpaints.com
Interior design by Velin@Perseus-Design.com

Paperback: ISBN: 978-1-78677-232-9
eBook: ISBN: 978-1-78677-233-6

Non-Fiction / BODY, MIND & SPIRIT / Parapsychology /
ESP, Clairvoyance, Precognition, Telepathy.

www.whitecrowbooks.com

Praise for
The Psi Mind in Action

"The Psi Mind calls for a theory of how human minds are able to impact the material world just with focused intention, including healing illness, since much empirical evidence proves the existence of these anomalous events. Robert Charman's book describes many of these verified and fascinating actions not explained by the materialist worldview. He includes observations and memories when the brain is technically dead, as during surgery, or group intention creating a thought form, or objects moved without human touch. Based on the evidence he describes, Charman suggests that a different "Psi Mind" state is associated with the power of mind able to impact matter, as when a healer's brain waves change during a healing session. He calls this the "two mind" approach, which is worthy of further scientific investigation. All the examples of "Psychokinetic effect" he includes are of interest and lead the readers to an expanded vision of reality and their own potential."

~ **Gayle Kimball, Ph.D.,** author of *Essential Energy Tools: How to Develop Your Clairvoyant and Healing Abilities, illustrative of the psi mind* and a trilogy of interview-based dialogues with visionary scientists: *The Mysteries of Reality, The Mysteries of Healing,* and *The Mysteries of Knowledge Beyond Our Senses.*

"*The Psi Mind in Action* by Robert Charman explores the ideas of a 'psi mind' and how this might be distinct from the normal everyday mind. Charman suggests that for psi effects and behaviours to be revealed, the individual needs to transition from the everyday conscious mind to the psi state of mind. That when this occurs, substantive evidence of psi effects and behaviours can be produced that is both beyond dispute and represents a serious challenge to current mainstream scientific thinking. To support these ideas Charman brings together a selection of intriguing evidence from an eclectic range of psi research. In particular, the evidence focuses on the idea of psi as an active agent. This evidence is further supported by the diligent examination of a number of case studies which take the reader on a useful and informative journey through the various ideas and processes involved. Overall, the book covers a range of issues in a clear and coherent manner, offering some unique and interesting insights, based on sound scientific data. It will not only inform but also stimulate the interested reader."

~ **Dr David Vernon,** Research Psychologist, holds a visiting senior lectureship at Canterbury Christ Church University, a research position at Derby University and is the author of the award-winning book *Dark Cognition: Evidence for psi and its implications for consciousness.*

"In a series of well-argued chapters, accessible to the general reader, Robert Charman draws on a wide range of topics which explore aspects of what he terms the 'psi mind'. This contrasts with our everyday state of mind in which we normally engage with the world around us through our senses. Rather, the psi mind is a relaxed condition which enables an influence to be exerted on other individuals, and even on physical objects. Its existence indicates that our minds are not passive recipients of information, capable only of acting on our bodies, but can extend beyond them.

His arguments are well-supported with references to reliable research, and the extensive evidence that has accumulated to support the existence of a psi mind is a challenge to mainstream science to address its implications. The underlying theme is the potential that lies untapped within the human mind, both to benefit the individual and the wider society. If the psi mind could be harnessed by greater numbers, it would improve the state of the world immeasurably.

The Psi Mind in Action challenges the conventional understanding of the mind's limited relationship with the wider environment and explores its complexity, which has barely been scratched. The notion of the psi mind suggests avenues for further exploration. Critics who wish to challenge Charman's thesis of the psi mind, and the evidence he presents to support its existence, will need to work hard to find valid counterarguments.

The reader will finish the book with a deeper understanding of well-attested phenomena pushing the boundaries of mainstream science: boundaries that will eventually have to be expanded to accommodate them."

~ **Dr Tom Ruffles,** Communications Officer, Society for Psychical Research and Honorary Visiting Research Fellow at Anglia Ruskin University, 2014-2019.

Grateful Acknowledgements

Firstly, to those intrepid researchers into psi phenomena, ignored and often wrongly vilified by their peers, whose empirical research findings into psi healing are clinically important and reviewed in the first two chapters of this book. Then to the wider world of the psi mind in action as covered in the rest of the book. As one interviewee said to a researcher, 'I know it can't have happened, so it didn't happen – but it did'. My theme in a nutshell.

Secondly, to Dr Malcolm Schofield, editor of the Society for Psychical Research peer reviewed Journal, and Dr Leo Ruckbie, editor of The Magazine of the Society for Psychical Research (formerly the Paranormal Review) for their encouragement and support, and Society members, especially Dr Tom Ruffles, for their appreciative comments over the years.

And thirdly, but most important personally, my thanks to my psychologist daughter, Dr Elizabeth Charman, for her invaluable academic critique of each chapter that has saved me from innumerable errors of commission and omission, and to Dr Richard Sugg, author of many highly reviewed books, both nonfiction and fiction, for his always helpful suggestions and careful correction of my many grammatical errors.

Contents

Praise for *The Psi Mind in Action* v

Grateful Acknowledgements ix

Introduction 1

1. Scientific Evidence for the Power of Psi Healing 11

2. EEG Studies Reveal That the Brainwaves of Healers and Patients Unite During Healing 39

3. Statistics Show Local Crime Waves Fall During Periods of Group Transcendental Meditation 55

4. Verified Out-of-Body Observations 73

5. Evidence That Personal Possessions can Mysteriously Disappear and Reappear, or Turn up Somewhere Else 93

6. Attempts to Conjure up a Ghost to be Called 'Philip' Show the Psychic Strength of the Group Mind 125

7. Acoustic Analysis Confirms the Temporary Existence of 'Eric' the Andover Wall Rapper 161

8. A Stolen Harp Found by Map Dowsing Leads to Dr Elizabeth Mayer's Revelatory Investigation into Psi Phenomena 179

9. Discussion. 219

Appendix A: Society for Psychical Research Presidents 241

Appendix B: Society for Psychical Research 245

References 251

Notes 269

About the Author 271

Introduction

"If you wish to upset the law that all crows are black, you mustn't seek to show that no crows are: it is enough if you prove one crow to be white."
~ Professor William James.
Presidential Address to the Society for Psychical Research 1896

The Psi Mind is the subject of this book, as it was in my previous book *Telepathy, Clairvoyance, and Precognition*. There is strong empirical as well as observational evidence of events and experiences that, according to mainstream science, cannot happen, and yet they have happened and they do happen, and they require an explanation (see Broderick and Goertzel, 2015, and Vernon, 2021).

The evidence-based chapters in this book show how the 'white crow' of psychical research has been demonstrated as a fact beyond all reasonable doubt: when people are in a 'psi' state of mind they can exert an effect on other living systems and affect physical objects. Those who believe that only non psi, black crows exist, and talk derisively of 'pseudoscience', or 'charlatans', or 'no scientific evidence', now have some very evidential psi white crows in their midst that will not fly away. The question is, given this empirical evidence, will the true scientific spirit of 'following where the evidence leads' now prevail in the scientific community? In my previous book I reviewed many case studies considered to be classic examples of different types of Extrasensory Perception (ESP). I sought to distinguish impartially between those cases best explained as a case of ESP, and those with a more likely, non-psi explanation. In that book the focus was on psi in receptive ESP mode, such as telepathy, clairvoyance and precognition. In this book the focus is on psi as an active agent capable of exerting an effect on the external world. This is known as the Psychokinetic (PK) effect.

There is empirical evidence that the psi mind can exert a PK effect on the metabolism of other living systems, as in psi healing, and can move physical objects. How it can do this will be known only when we know how our mentality interacts with the physical world. It should be remembered that the 'you are your brain' theory that so dominates the neurosciences at present, is not a statement of empirical fact, but a strongly held belief. It is based upon known correlations between areas of brain activity and reported mental activity. This is invaluable clinical information, so, for all practical purposes, this theory works very well. But 'correlation' is not 'explanation' as to cause. The 'brain is mind' theory hides the fact that no one has any idea how the physical brain, with its endless streams of bioelectrical impulses travelling around the brain at different frequencies, can possibly be the mentality that is 'you' and 'me'. The physical brain and its billions of brain cells, or neurons, cannot experience hate, love, fears, emotions, and ambitions any more than the electronic circuits in a computer or smartphone. Brains cannot love or hate other brains. Physics, whether classical or quantum, has no equation for mentality because there is no physical unit of mentality. Our complete ignorance of the nature of the brain/mind relationship can be summed up by the following aphorism: "The neurologist can explain neurology, but neurology cannot explain the neurologist."

In the first chapter of the book I include details of a major trial demonstrating the profound symptom relief felt by patients when they receive what I have termed as 'psi healing'. This is followed by other clinical examples, including the case study of a patient diagnosed with terminal lung cancer who obtained a complete cure coincident with receiving psi healing. Despite medical science consigning such outcomes as a 'placebo effect' based on patients' prior beliefs that they will experience relief as a result of healing, there is a large number of controlled studies showing that this is not a sufficient explanation. Some of the more striking of these non-placebo studies (i.e., where no prior belief is possible) are discussed in this chapter. These include evidence that psi healing can accelerate normal cell metabolism, accelerate the multiplication rate of tissue cell grown in cultures, and accelerate the rate of tissue healing. It can inhibit cancer cell growth, increase the death rate of cancer cells, and has ensured survival of mice injected with a fatal form of cancer. Other studies have shown that psi healing can increase the processes of seed germination and the growth rate of seedlings, and inhibit bacterial growth. The findings of these non-placebo studies indicate that psi healing can exert a direct effect at bodily tissue level as well as providing mental relief.

Chapter 2 then focuses on the relationship between healers and clients in a healing session, providing a review of joint healer/client EEG studies. These studies show that when a healer is in the 'psi healing mindset' their brain waves show a typical frequency profile that remains steady and can be displayed on a monitor screen. During a healing session the brain waves of their client, or healee, come into a similar frequency profile with the healer's profile as if entrained, and then diverge once the healing is over. This implies that healer and healee are as one during the healing session.

Chapter 3 presents sociological studies demonstrating that when practitioners of Transcendental Meditation, or TM-Sidhi, are in twice daily group meditation over an extended period, there is a co-incident drop in local official crime statistics, and population surveys record increased feelings of happiness and wellbeing in the community. It seems that when TM-Sidhi practitioners are in this form of the psi mind, their deep meditation can subconsciously affect people living in the surrounding area. TM-Sidhi meditators believe that when they are in a state of deep meditation they become as one with the Universal Field of Pure Consciousness in which we are all immersed.

Chapter 4 looks at a different type of psi phenomenon: the Out-of-Body Experience (OBE).

When a person has an OBE they experience a very compelling sensation that they have left their body and are looking down at it, or observing what is happening elsewhere. This is difficult enough to explain when the person is conscious while having the experience. The real problem is how to explain an OBE when a person is unconscious following, say, a cardiac arrest, or when anaesthetised during an operation, or kept under sedation following a brain injury. They are lying flat on their back with eyes shut, often taped shut during surgery, and often not responsive to any form of painful stimuli. Yet there are hundreds of cases where patients, on recovery, describe what they observed during their OBE that can be verified by those present at the scene. I have proposed that an OBE occurs during a brief moment of brain consciousness when the psi mind is the conscious witness.

Introduction

Chapter 5 explores two explanations for a common experience that we might not even consider a 'psi' phenomenon. We all mislay small personal possessions, and either find them again or not at all. But what about when those possessions disappear, only to reappear in the same place or somewhere else that is just not possible? Or are replaced by something similar that you don't recognise? It just doesn't make everyday sense, so, with an irritable shrug, you eventually give up trying to explain it and dismiss your experience as 'just one of those things'. This chapter discusses the work of two researchers who have collected hundreds of carefully evaluated examples of this type of phenomenon. They suggest that when such events happen, something fundamental has occurred in the human mind/matter relationship.

Chapters 6 and 7 move on to consider another type of psi mind phenomenon, where there seems to be a psychokinetic interaction with physical objects. Chapter 6 presents the intriguing story of eight members of the Toronto Society of Psychical Research who tried to conjure up a ghost they intended to call 'Philip'. Following a year of fruitless endeavour, something did happen, but not what they expected. Whilst they were unable to conjure up 'Philip' as a mid-air ghost, instead, 'Philip' as a group psi mind creation unexpectedly 'inhabited' a table during their group sessions, answering questions by rapping, and causing the table to career round the room with them in tow. In between sessions it was just an ordinary table. This sensational, psychokinetic phenomenon was captured in full detail in two films as well by Toronto television.

Chapter 7 describes the story of 'Eric' the Andover wall rapper which, in its strange way, is even more mysterious. For some eight weeks in 1974 he 'lived' in a bedroom wall of a family home. He said his name was Eric, and he communicated with the family by the sound of raps coming from the wall in answer to their questions. Not only that, but sometimes he became angry and banged so loudly that people in the street could hear him. Dr Barrie Colvin, who investigated the case, recorded Eric's answering raps together with normal knuckle taps on the wall for acoustic comparison. When the two sets were subjected to acoustic analysis, the Eric raps were quite different in acoustic waveform profile from taps when the wall was knocked. This objective difference confirmed Eric's temporary existence, but provided no clue as to what or who he was. Maybe 'he' had something to do with someone in the family, for some unexplained reason. But if so, what?

Chapter 8 takes the reader into the wider world of psi phenomena as discovered by psychologist and psychoanalyst Dr Elizabeth Mayer, Associate Clinical Professor of Psychology, University of California. It all started with the remarkable story of how her daughter's harp, stolen during a 1991 Christmas concert in Oakland, California, was located at a specific house in Oakland by Major Harold McCoy, while map dowsing in Fayetteville, Arkansas, some 1,800 miles away. After Dr Mayer had negotiated its recovery, she was so stunned by how it had been located that she said, "I had to face the fact that my notions of space, time, reality, and the nature of the human mind were stunningly inadequate." She then embarked on extensive investigation into psi phenomena, including four reputable psychics who described how they left their everyday state of mind to enter into a 'psi' state of mind to do accurate readings of their clients, even when their clients were hundreds of miles away. After presenting the positive findings of her research across a wide spectrum of psi phenomena, she discusses a theory, involving a possible relationship between psi and quantum reality.

INTRODUCTION

The psi hypothesis

The more cases of extrasensory perception (ESP) I have read, the more I have noticed that when people report a psi experience they also comment that they seemed to be in a different state of mind from their everyday mind. This is mentioned again and again, often in a puzzled 'I felt strangely different' sort of way. Being in this different state of mind when having, for example, a precognition, seems a constant feature.

In my previous book, *Telepathy, Clairvoyance and Premonition*, I proposed that there are two separate states of mind: the everyday, non psi, state of mind, and the psi state of mind. The everyday state of mind relies on information about the outside world as impulses stream into the brain through the sensory nervous system, as in sight, sound and touch, and acts upon the outside world through bodily activity. When in this state of mind the occurrence of ESP or PK is very unlikely as this mindset recognises bodily input only. However, when someone transitions from the everyday state into the psi state of mind, their mental reality changes completely. Information as in telepathy, clairvoyance, and precognition is obtained directly when in the psi state of mind and, as recounted in this book, the psi mind can exert an external psychokinetic effect. This implies that the two states of mind have different properties appropriate to their role in our lives.

During consciousness, both states of mind exert a controlling, purpose driven, psychokinetic influence on the brain and, reciprocally, the brain exerts a neuro-kinetic influence on the mind through sensory input. In the everyday state of mind this reciprocity is total and controls all that one can know about the external world and how to physically interact with it. But when in the psi state the mind is released from such total reciprocity. ESP becomes the informational norm and the PK effect on other living systems and physical objects becomes possible.

This is not offered as an explanation because, as already mentioned, we have no explanations for the everyday state of consciousness, let alone the psi state of consciousness. What we have, in both cases, are consistent correlations between two different forms of mental activity, either with the everyday world or with psi phenomena. If this two-states-of-mind hypothesis is correct, it may explain why so many experiments designed to detect telepathic or clairvoyant abilities have attained borderline statistical significance or null results. Volunteers (often cohorts of students) have remained in their everyday state of mind, consciously willing success, and only the occasional star performer has, unknowingly, transitioned into a psi state of mind. What often happens is that their successful results, known as 'dazzle shots', become merged into the overall statistics of the group, or considered as chance outliers, so it appears that the study has 'failed' and the opportunity to follow up is missed.

A final comment

Whether you agree with this proposed two mind hypothesis or not, I think, like me, you will be intrigued by the objective evidence for the external psychokinetic effect. The clinical implications of the first two chapters on psi healing, and healer/healee unity during healing, are considerable and require mainstream research, as does the TM-Sidhi effect. The evidence for psi, whether in the receptive form of ESP as explored in my previous book, or as an agent of external psychokinetic effect as presented in this book, is beyond reasonable dispute. The real problem is how to explain it.

Introduction

Note: Many of the chapters in this book are based upon papers published either by the peer reviewed *journal of the Society for Psychical Research*, or its companion Paranormal Review magazine (now The Magazine of the Society for Psychical Research).

1

Scientific Evidence for the Power of Psi Healing

This chapter is divided into two parts. Part One discusses the welcome symptom relief experienced by patients during and after receiving psi healing, and Part Two presents experimental studies demonstrating that this relief may be based on far more than 'just placebo' effect. There is empirical evidence that when healers are in the psi healing state of mind their healing intention can influence the metabolic processes of cells and tissues directly. These findings imply that psi healing can be considered as a therapeutic agent in its own right.

PART ONE: SYMPTOM RELIEF

Psi Healing

The term 'psi healing' is used here as a generic term covering different healer belief systems such as Psychic Healing, Spiritual Healing, Reiki, Johrei, Qigong, BioEnergy Healing, Energy Healing, Therapeutic Touch, and The Bengston Energy Healing Method. Although healer practitioners may differ in their belief as to its nature, source and mode of action, they share a common belief that the practice of healing involves the transmission of 'healing energy' from or through the healer into the client or patient in response to their physical and/or mental needs. Bengston (see Part Two) refers to it as a bioinformation field. Psi healers often experience what they interpret as an 'energy flow' along their arms with a sensation of heat or tingling in their hands and fingers, and the person receiving healing often describe a feeling of warmth, as if the 'healing energy' is flowing into their body under the hands of the healer, even when not in physical contact. This relaxing sensation is often accompanied by a profound sense of relief from physical and mental distress (Moga, 2017).

A typical healing session

During a healing session, which usually lasts between 20-30 minutes, the patient, who remains fully clothed, either sits in a comfortable chair or lies on a couch, either on their back or face down according to which position is most comfortable, with their eyes closed. Sometimes, if they wish, soft background music is played. The healer then quietly moves round the patient, often starting at the head, then moving down over the throat, heart, and abdomen, then along the arms and legs, finishing at the feet: often holding their hands stationary for a minute or so over each major area, or longer over a particularly painful area. They either hold their hands a few inches above the body as they move round or, with permission, place their hands very lightly on the patient. After the healing session has ended, the patient remains still for a few minutes, then takes their time to leave.

Whatever their condition, be it arthritis, backache or some other disability, most patients report feeling a profound sense of relaxation, with the pain and aching dying away. They often feel warmth or tingling under the healer's hands, even when they are not being touched, and many report seeing peaceful images floating into their minds as they relax. This improvement tends to be sustained during follow-up healing sessions.

Psi healing relief for IBS and IBD sufferers

A major study into the effect of psi healing for patients suffering from chronic irritable bowel syndrome (IBS) and inflammatory bowel disease (IBD) was conducted by Dr Sukhdev Singh, Senior Consultant in Gastroenterology, Good Hope Hospital, Sutton Coldfield, and Senior Lecturer, University of Birmingham Medical School, in association with the University of Birmingham Medical School with Sandy Edwards as Lead Healer. It was funded by a £250,000 grant from the National Lottery. Enrolled into the trial were 200 patients: 100 patients suffering from chronic IBS and 100 patients suffering from chronic IBD, with the latter including ulcerative colitis and Crohn's disease. While continuing with their normal medical management, they received a 20–30-minute session of healing once a week for five consecutive weeks. The patients acted as their own comparative symptom control, using specially designed Measure Yourself Medical Outcomes Profile (MYMOP) Quality of Life (QoL) questionnaires. They completed them during weeks before receiving healing, during the five-week session of healing, and for the following 24 weeks follow-up. The scoring of the two sets were then compared. The healers were members of the National Federation of Spiritual Healers (now the Healing Trust), and patients were seen in a consulting room.

Results

The researchers found that there was a significant improvement in the MYMOP score at week 6 ($p < 0.001$) which was maintained to week 12 ($p < 0.001$) and 24 ($p < 0.001$). Improvements in MYMOP were significantly greater in the intervention group at both 6 ($p < 0.001$) and 12 weeks ($p < 0.001$) with effect sizes of 0.7 (95% CI: 0.4–1.1) and 0.8 (95% CI: 0.4–1.2). Condition-specific data for IBS showed that most QoL dimensions had a significant minimum 10-point score improvement at 6 and 12 weeks. In IBD there was also similar score improvement, but only up to week 12 were there associations of improved social and bowel functions ($p < 0.001$, respectively). Based on these data, the researchers were able to conclude that the addition of healing therapy to conventional treatment was associated with improvement in symptoms and QoL, including engagement in social activities and work in IBS patients, and to a lesser extent in IBD patients. (See Lee, Kingston, Roberts *et al.*, 2017 for quantitative analysis, and Soundy, Lee, Kingstone *et al.* 2015, for qualitative analysis).

Some comments made by patients during the IBS/IBD trial

"I felt great comfort when the healer's hands were on my lower belly. I feel marvellous."

"I felt benefit immediately."

"I now have total peace of mind. I was very stressed and agitated beforehand."

"I felt totally blessed. I feel completely destressed now."

"It felt really good. There was a warmth, like a warm drink, in my lower belly, just like the Ready Brek advert. Really enjoyable, like being in a different world. Really relaxed. I thought I was peaceful when I arrived but, during the session, I realised I was releasing tensions."

"Brilliant. I was aware of a sudden release of tension in the pelvic area."

"It was very warm wherever the healer was working. The stomach ache I came in with has gone and I feel relaxed."

"This was a magical experience and helped a great deal because the pain has literally gone."

"Bizarre! I didn't expect healing to work as well as it did. I felt tingly mostly in my hands and both arms. I loved it!"

"It took a while for me to switch off, but then I was able to relax fully for deeper and longer than I can remember. I feel more positive now. I felt warmth in my legs during the session."

"Halfway through the session, I felt heat and comfort in the pelvic cradle that became more intense. I became the most relaxed that I have ever been in my life."

These comments in response to the QoL interviews are taken from dozens more as recorded by Sandy Edwards in her 2017 book *Healing in a Hospital: Scientific Evidence that Spiritual Healing improves Health*. Very importantly, she describes her own journey into healing, first as a healer in general practice, then healing in a hospital. She includes a review on the numerous studies demonstrating the positive effects of healing, and takes the reader through the trials and tribulations of setting up and running a clinical trial and analysing the results.

Healer, Angie Buxton-King

Angie Buxton-King was lead healer of a team of NHS employed psi healers in the children and adult oncology wards of University College London Hospital (UCLH) for many years. In her two books *The NHS Healer: How My Son's Life Inspired a Healing Journey* (2004), and *The NHS Healer: Onwards and Upwards* (2017), she presents many case histories of significant symptom relief from cancer, together with reduced side effects of chemotherapy and radiotherapy.

As with the IBS/IBD study, this relief was experienced just as frequently by adult patients who, despite their personal lack of belief in healing, had agreed to see a healer in response to urging from friends or relatives. On this issue of whether belief or no belief affects client response, psi healer Matthew Manning (1997) states that from his records he found that lack of belief made little difference as to the degree of symptom relief, unexpected remission or even cure of a particular illness, that occurs coincident with receiving healing. This implies that the effects of psi healing are not limited to mental expectation only; but more of that later. Here are a few typical comments from patients on receiving psi healing, taken from Buxton-King's second book:

> "The abdominal pains I had have now disappeared."
> "I can't believe that my sickness has gone away."
> "That was really lovely and so relaxing. It helped with my breathing."

"Very odd – never had Reiki before. I was feeling so nauseous beforehand and it has completely disappeared."

"My God – that was incredible. I was uncertain about having treatment but that was so relaxing."

"That has really helped with my pain."

"I don't understand it, but if it works it works – and it works!"

"My husband tells everyone about you – he was in so much pain, but after he saw you it disappeared and has never come back."

From her second book, under the heading of 'My Experience of Healing in the NHS' (pp. 144-150) we hear from consultant anaesthetist Dr Anil Wijetunge, diagnosed as suffering from acute lymphoblastic leukaemia. After undergoing months of intensive chemotherapy and full body radiation, Dr Wijetunge describes the contribution psi healing made to his recovery. Emaciated, feeling really ill, suffering from acutely painful 'golf ball sized' skin eruptions, repeated chest infections and a patella that had necrosed and was too painful for morphine to fully control, he was asked if he would like to see a healer. Despite his orthodox medical belief that a so-called healer moving their hands in the air around his body could not possibly have any pain relieving effect whatsoever, he agreed as he was beyond arguing. During the first treatment, as the healer's hands slowly moved over his head and then down across his body to his feet in a series of paused stages, he says "I felt that I was no longer in the isolation room but moving through a most beautiful garden full of light, colour and peace. ... All was calm and there was no discomfort or pain now ... I felt genuine happiness." He continued receiving 30 minutes of weekly healing, with similar levels of symptom relief and mental relaxation, until he was discharged home after his condition had improved to the point of receiving a successful stem cell transplant. In retrospect he says that "Reiki healing provided me with a much-needed place of refuge, calm and beauty from the pain and discomforts of illness."

A case study

This seems to be an appropriate place to include the following case study. Donald Clark, a patient with a prognosis of late stage, terminal, lung cancer, attended for once weekly psi healing over a number of weeks. During that time, and medically speaking co-incidentally, his lung cancer commenced to regress, and eventually went into complete remission and medically confirmed cure. He had fully accepted his consultant's prognosis that his cancer had now entered a terminal stage of inevitable progression to death, and as he possessed no belief whatsoever in what he termed as 'the nonsense' of healers and healing, his expectation was near zero.

Here is his story as told to reporter Julie Cohen (1997).

> In September 1994, Donald Clark, a retired electrician aged 68, divorced, living on his own in Bromley, Kent, UK, and an ex 20 a day smoker for 50 years, was feeling increasingly tired and unwell with a persistent cough and shortness of breath. Radiographs showed that he had malignant lung cancer, and, despite receiving two courses of radiotherapy, the cancer continued to spread. He was offered chemotherapy as a last resort, but, after speaking to patients who were undergoing chemotherapy for the same type of cancer, he decided not to take up the offer. By late spring 1995 the proliferation of cancer throughout

both lungs was increasing at such a rate that his consultant referred him to a local hospice with a terminal prognosis of around eight months. As Clark says "No one can describe how it feels to be told you have eight months to live. I felt a mixture of anger and terror." After visiting the hospice several times Clark decided not to move in as "I couldn't come to terms with going somewhere to die." As breathing became increasingly difficult, and walking distance was reduced to a few yards before having to stop and recover his breath, he says that he felt "mentally and physically demoralised."

Seeing his distress and despair and desperate to help, his daughter suggested that he saw a healer, so to please her despite having no faith in "such nonsense" he booked a session at a nearby healing centre manned by members of the then National Federation of Spiritual Healers (now The Healing Trust). On his first visit he was disappointed to see nothing more impressive than "a room with just a few chairs". He sat down, and after he had told the healer of his terminal prognosis "She placed her hands a few inches away from my chest and then around my body. I felt a warm tingling sensation but nothing really dramatic." For the first three to four weeks he did not notice any difference in what he could do following his weekly, half hour sessions "but as I didn't expect it to work anyway I was not surprised." He did, however, notice that he felt very relaxed during and after each healing session which was a real relief in itself, and his daughter said he was definitely looking better "but I thought she was talking rubbish."

However, despite his disbelief, he noticed that he could get dressed without stopping for breath, and walk further without becoming breathless, and within a few weeks he was able to walk to nearby shops and carry his shopping home. At the same time he found that he had more energy, was sleeping better, eating better, and feeling better than he had for years. His quarterly chest x rays showed that against all clinical prognosis for his type of late stage lung cancer, the tumours were steadily shrinking and eventually became non detectable.

Two years later in September, 1997, he required a medical certificate for health insurance to cover a holiday abroad. Radiographs confirmed that no tumour was present, and accordingly he received full insurance cover. At the time of interview he said that "Over the past year I've felt fitter and healthier than I have for ten years. I'm even able to work again and I now help organise a charity shop. I went to a healer only because I had nothing to lose, but I'm now convinced there are people with extraordinary gifts that can help."

A medical perspective on the results of psi healing

Medically speaking, Donald Clark's recovery from a prognosis of terminal lung cancer falls under the heading of 'spontaneous remission' of unknown cause. His attendance for healing would be seen as purely co-incidental and any mental relief that he felt classed as a 'placebo effect' – i.e., based on a belief in healing, rather than any active effect from the healing itself. Indeed, trials have shown that feelings of pain, aching, fatigue and mental distress can be markedly reduced by belief in whatever is being offered, and this relief in turn causes the brain to release natural pain relieving endorphins and reduce the output of stress hormones.

Thus, from a medical perspective, psi healing falls under the definition of a placebo, because waving hands over someone's body, or lightly touching them, can no more have a direct effect on the physical cause of the illness or disease itself than a chalk tablet because there is no possible mechanism. Mental intention, whatever the state of mind of the intentioner, cannot have an external, objective effect. In clinical medicine, the treatment of the cause of bodily illness is by drugs that can act directly on the pathological processes, as in antibiotics, or chemotherapy to kill cancer cells, or by radiotherapy to destroy cancer cells, or in surgical removal. Placebo effects cannot treat pathological cause; they act as a temporary mental bonus.

Healers take on the challenge of the medical perspective

Centuries of historical narration up to the present day have included verified cases of healers curing the apparently terminal sick, or recovering lost senses as in sight and hearing, or enabling people to walk again. In the 20th century, healers in the UK organised themselves into organisations such as the National Society Federation of Spiritual Healers (NSFSH), the Confederation of Healing Organisations (CHO), or Reiki organisations, with a training programme, qualifications, professional standards governing practice, and a complaints procedure. Their claims that when in the mindset of healing they could relieve physical diseases and disabilities beyond any placebo explanation drew increasing professional curiosity. From the 1960s to the present day, randomised controlled trials have been designed to put such claims to the test. Perhaps the most compelling of these are tests of psi healing using animals, plants, cell and tissue cultures where the 'placebo effect' is not a possible explanation. These positive results from these 'non-placebo' studies challenge mainstream assumptions that mental intention, as in psi healing, cannot have an external effect.

The results of this non placebo research forms the subject of Part Two, starting with the remarkable series of experiments carried out by Dr William Bengston, Sociology lecturer, St Joseph's College, New York.

PART TWO: NON-PLACEBO RESEARCH

The mice that did not die

In the early 1970s, while working as a pool lifeguard in New York after taking his first degree and then studying for his masters, William Bengston met ex American army veteran Bennett Mayrick, who claimed to be a healer. Initially very sceptical of such a claim, Bengston became impressed by the many accounts that Mayrick was receiving from clients who, after receiving a diagnosis of cancer and then receiving psi healing before medical treatment started, had been told that repeat tests showed their cancer had disappeared. He decided to put these anecdotal reports to a replicable test using mice injected with a fatal form of mammary cancer cells. They would either survive or die.

With Dr David Krinsley, then Head of Geology, Queen's College, City University, New York, Bengston devised a test that he considered to be as near foolproof as one could get. A strain of laboratory mice that is fatally susceptible to injections of mammary adenocarcinoma cells was chosen for the study. Without known exception they die within 14 to 27 days after receiving the adenocarcinoma cell injection.

Scientific Evidence for the Power of Psi Healing

Following injection of the first six experimental mice the study was about to commence when Mayrick suddenly backed out, saying that as he already knew healing worked he was not interested in doing a trial. With no alternative healer available, Bengston, who had no belief in possessing any healing ability but had evolved a pre-healing mental preparation technique with Mayrick to enhance its effects, became the healer. After mentally going through the pre-healing technique, he put his hands on each side of their cage for an hour each day of the study.

During each session he found, much to his surprise, that his left hand felt hot as if energy was running through it, then through the mice in the cage into his right hand, and back up his arm through his brain. He had assumed that if psi healing worked then no cancer tumour would develop but, to his horror, the tumours on the sides of the mice grew in size, black areas appeared and then ulcerated. Despite these outer cancerous changes, the eyes of the mice remained bright, their coats beyond the edge of the tumour remained smooth, and they continued eating and running around as normal. The tumours then imploded around the 35th day with no discharge or infection; the area closed and their skin and fur regrew. Cancer remission was complete and the mice continued to live their natural lifespan of two years. For the first time in history, members of this strain of mammary cancer susceptible mice had lived beyond 27 days and returned to a full state of health.

Once the mice had fully recovered it was found that they remained immune to further injections of the same cancer. If their white cells were extracted and injected into other mice who had received a normally fatal cancer cell injection, immunity was conferred and no cancer developed. It seemed that in response to the animals' acute survival need, psi healing had somehow effected a reprogramming of their immune system to recognise and kill the cancer cells. Psi healing had effectively 'vaccinated' the mice against this particular form of cancer and, in turn, mice injected with their immune cells were vaccinated as well.

Of particular interest was the behaviour of the mice during each study. In his first study Bengston noted that the mice all crowded to the left-hand side of the cage to expose their growing tumour to his left hand that, as he said, was feeling hot as if energy was running through it. But once the tumour had imploded, and that area was now healing, they ran around as usual. The same behaviour was noted in subsequent trials using volunteer psi healers that Bengston had trained in his pre-healing technique.

Another unexpected finding was that if healers, still in the psi healing mindset, broke experimental protocol and visited the injected control mice housed in another area of the laboratory to see how they were faring, those mice still alive at the time of their visit also survived. Bengston (2017) has now repeated these successful findings in sixteen controlled trials conducted in four university laboratories and four medical school laboratories using students trained in his Bengston Energy Healing® technique.[1]

A chance, but crucially important finding, was that when some biology students trained in the Bengston technique were apparently healing their mice by placing their hands on each side of their cage, but at the same time were feeling embarrassed and self-conscious when doing this publicly in the laboratory, those mice died as if they had not received psi healing, just like the untreated controls. But when the same students treated their mice in the relaxed privacy of their rooms, those mice survived (Bengston, 2019).

---

[1] See Bengston's website http://www.bengstonresearch.com/ for free article downloads, CDs describing his pre-healing technique, photographs of the mice before and after psi healing, and latest research into how psi healing may work.

The implication of this observation is that to survive their cancer, the mice depended upon their healer being in the full psi healing state of mind untroubled by self-doubt. This raises the question of what distinguishes the psi healing state of mind from the everyday non-psi state of mind. How, in this case, does it successfully activate the immune system of the mouse to recognise and destroy carcinoma cells and remain cancer free? What is the nature of the relationship, between the psi healing mindset and the sick mouse, that effects recovery? These questions have yet to be answered. Traditionally, because this is how it feels to them, healers believe they act as the conduit through whom 'healing energy' is transmitted into the patient. In his review of his research findings concerning these mice with cancer and a range of other clinical conditions Bengston (2019) tentatively interprets this healing relationship more in the form of a bio-information field acting as a bond between healer and healee, whether mouse or human, in which the healer in their receptive psi healing mindset senses and responds to the survival needs of the healee. In the case of the mice, their survival need was for their immune system to recognise and kill the cancer cells.

Institutional resistance

Despite observing these consistently successful results, each of the laboratories in which these trials were performed has refused permission for long term follow-up experiments. In 2010 Bengston summarised this depressing experience by saying that "Each new lab expresses disbelief at my data obtained in other labs and their researchers take the 'Oh yeah, well you couldn't get these results here' approach. When the mice get cured in the first experiment it is usually taken as a gauntlet by lab personnel that they can thwart future results. Then, when the second experiment produces full lifespan cures, it is often followed by head shaking and proclamations to the effect that this is the most amazing thing they have ever seen. But when I suggest further research there is always some reason that the work cannot continue at that institution" (Bengston, 2010, p6) and nothing seems to have changed. Considering the reasons for this reaction Bengston comments that "All fields of science – physics, chemistry, biology- fiercely protect their orthodoxies. Any findings that don't fit are deemed not to have happened" (Bengston, 2010, p160).

Of his experience treating clients who came to him through informal recommendation Bengston (2010, p9) says that

> Over the past thirty-five years I've successfully treated many types of cancer – bone, pancreatic, breast, brain, rectal, lymphatic, stomach and leukaemia – as well as other diseases, all using a hands-on technique that is painless, non-invasive, and has no unpleasant side effects. To my knowledge, no person I have healed has ever experienced a re-occurrence.

To his surprise the most aggressive forms of cancer were the cancers most susceptible to psi healing. By 2010 this anecdotal reportage of psi healing effectiveness had "been proven in ten controlled animal experiments conducted in five university medical and biological laboratories by trained, initially sceptical researchers." At the time Bengston commented that "Though my initial response to the validity of hands-on healing was one of incredulity, the accumulation of replicable scientific data has overwhelmed my own disbelief. I have become a failed sceptic" (p 9). Despite writing his book and publishing his research online, there has been no response from the medical community.

Psi healing accelerates cell multiplication rates compared with controls

In 2008 Dr Gloria A. Gronowicz, who gained her PhD in molecular and cell biology, and is currently Professor of Surgery at the Departments of Surgery and Orthopaedics, University of Connecticut Health Centre, Farmington, published the results of an important study in which three types of body cells grown in tissue cultures multiplied faster when exposed to periods of healing intention compared with controls (Gronowicz, 2008). These results, like Bengston's remarkable findings of cancer cure, and the many research references to follow, challenge orthodox scientific theory that mental intention cannot objectively affect the outside world.

The experiment

The two-year-long study consisted of growing separate cultures of bone cells (osteoblasts), tendon cells (tenocytes), and fibroblasts (cells that synthesise the soft tissues under the skin and are essential to wound healing) in a standardised nutrient medium. Each of the three different types of cell were divided into three cultures. Culture A was exposed to healing intention, culture B was exposed to sham healing, and culture C acted as the untreated control.

The cultures were brought out of an incubator, ring clamped onto 15-inch high stands mounted on a laboratory bench for ten minutes where they were subject to healing intention, sham healing or untreated as described below, and returned to the incubator. Standard laboratory assays were performed at the end of the first week and second week to assess the rate of cell proliferation in each culture. This experimental procedure was repeated many times with many different samples of each of the three types of cell.

The same three registered nurses, who had been trained in the healing technique known as Therapeutic Touch (TT), were involved throughout the study. Before each session they practised a meditative technique in which they removed everyday worries and concerns from their mind, and then 'centred' their minds into a quiet, healing mindset. When they felt ready to heal they rested their arms on the bench, held their hands about four inches (100cm) away from the cell culture on its 15-inch stand, and directed positive intention for the good health of the cells during each ten minute session. For culture B sham healing, technicians from other departments who did not know the purpose of the experiment, sat in the same position, and were asked to count backwards from 1000 to prevent any directed thought. Culture C was just brought out of the incubator, placed in the bench stand for 10 minutes, and then returned to the incubation unit.

Results

The findings were clear cut. When the cell proliferation rates for each of the three cultures were compared, those cultures exposed to the ten minute periods of healing intention demonstrated a consistent and significantly greater rate of cell proliferation than those in either the sham culture or control culture. In fact, the proliferation rates for the latter two groups were almost indistinguishable from each other. It was found that just two exposures of healing intention per week over two weeks were enough to stimulate a significant degree of cell proliferation. During trials in which the frequency of exposure to healing was increased it was found that each type of cell showed a different dosage response, so in that sense standard 'doses' of healing intention acted in a similar way to standard dosages of normal substances under test. While TT practitioners were used in this trial, the results would probably have been the same if they had been trained in Reiki or any other form of healing practice. It is important to note that as there was no significant difference in cell proliferation rates between the two control cultures, the psi healing state of mind was the effective mental agent in every trial.

The findings of this study from a reputable institution with a proven research record would have been accepted without question if the cells had been irradiated by, say, red light, as absorption of electromagnetic (em) frequencies in the red light spectrum is known to increase the rate of cell metabolism and consequent cell proliferation. There are, therefore, no valid scientific reasons to dismiss these findings when informed that the agent under test was the application of healing intention to the cell culture across space by three registered nurses who had been trained in Therapeutic Touch. Nevertheless, such is the strength of orthodox opinion, that despite the fact that these experiments followed standard experimental protocol and analysis and were repeated many times, the findings have been rejected.

In their discussion the authors refer to previous studies investigating cellular responses to directed healing intention. One study (Kiang *et al.* 2002) found increases in intracellular calcium ion concentrations, known to stimulate cell metabolic rates when exposed to 'bioenergy induction' as a neutral term for healing intention. A study using Reiki practitioners found increased survival and growth of bacteria in heat shocked bacterial cultures compared with controls (Rubik *et al.* (2006)). Yu *et al.* (2003) found that cultures of PC3, a human prostate cancer cell line, showed significantly decreased growth and multiplication rate during 48 hours of sustained negative intention by a Buddhist Zen Master compared with controls.

In a review of studies assessing the effect of the application of 'external qi' (healing energy generated and directed outwards from the healer) on cancer cell cultures, derived from breast, liver, lung, and bone marrow, Chen (2004) found significant inhibition of cancer cell proliferation. Such findings imply that directed healing intention under various belief systems including 'bioenergies' or 'external qi', can have a measurable effect on cell metabolism and somehow stimulate healthy cells that would be involved in bodily repair to proliferate and, importantly, to inhibit abnormal cancer cell activity.

Other non-placebo studies

Dr Bernard Grad, a Canadian biologist at McGill University, Montreal, measured the rate of skin healing in mice following surgically created 1cm superficial skin wounds on their backs. One group of mice was exposed to daily psi healing by the Hungarian healer Oskar Esterbany while placing his hands on each side of their cage, with another group of mice acting as non-exposed controls. Over the following fourteen days the skin wounds of the mice exposed to psi healing healed more quickly than the controls (Grad, Cadoret & Paul, 1961, Grad, 1965). A similar acceleration of skin wound healing in wounds exposed to psi healing compared with controls was found by de Souza *et al.* (2017) in a repeat study using rats. In another series of experiments using Esterbany as the healer, the rate of seed germination and seedling plant growth exposed to psi healing consistently exceeded that of control groups (Grad, 1963, 1964). For an overview of studies using Oskar Esterbany, see Grad (1965).

In all these studies the effect of psi healing appears to have been one of enhancing those metabolic activities favouring survival outcomes, rate of growth or rate of healing. Studies of the effect of psi healing on cancer cell cultures when the psi intention has been to inhibit cell proliferation have demonstrated both an inhibition of cell proliferation and acceleration of cancer cell death compared with controls (Shah *et al.*, 2011, Monzillo & Gronowicz, 2011, Trivedi *et al.* (2015, Yount *et al.*, 2012). Nash (1982) found a significant reduction in the rate of bacterial proliferation in infectious bacterial cultures exposed to negative psi intention, that is, to inhibit bacterial proliferation, compared with controls.

Smith (1968, 1972) and Rein (1978) found that enzyme reactions were accelerated in flasks held by healers compared with those held by controls. Bunnell (1996, 1999) found an increase in the rate of peptic enzyme breakdown of a standardised solution of egg albumen in those tubes exposed to psi healing compared with non-exposed controls.

A lettuce seed survival study

A recent non-placebo study ((de Milo *et al.*, 2021) has also demonstrated an effect beyond chance. This study evaluated the effect of Johrei healing on "sustaining the physiological potential of lettuce seeds" after receiving healing from Johrei practitioners compared with untreated controls. Johrei is a spiritual healing practice based on the focussing of universal life energy, also referred to as divine or spiritual light, through the palms of the hands across space into the healee. In this study, all the lettuce seeds were first subjected to the same level of potentially damaging heat stress with one group of seeds receiving Johrei healing immediately afterwards. Both groups of seeds were then kept in cold storage for two years. On being taken out of storage the same group of seeds again received Johrei healing. Both groups were then sown in an identical nutrient medium and assessed for percentage of seed germination, the rate of germination, the percentage of viable seedlings, and comparative root and shoot dry mass. For each variable under test the Johrei treated group demonstrated greater recovery, greater growth rates, and a larger dry mass compared with the untreated group at a statistical level of $p<0.001$. The authors concluded that Johrei had "effectively preserved lettuce seed health" during the two years of storage after being heat stressed.

Recent cancer studies

American scientist Dr Shamina Jain obtained her BA degree in Neuroscience and Behaviour at Columbia University, her MA degree in Integrative Health Psychology at the University of Arizona and her PhD in Clinical Psychology and Psychoneuroimmunology from San Diego State University. Her book *Healing Ourselves: Biofield Science and the Future of Health* (2021), is based on peer reviewed research findings into complementary, or biofield, therapies. She devotes Chapter 8, Healing Down to Our Cells, to a review of the laboratory findings of the specific effects of psi healing on cellular metabolism at DNA cell nucleus level in normal cells and cancer cells. The studies concentrated on a group of enzymes called protein kinases that regulate the activities of proteins involved in cell growth and repair, rates of cell division and programmed timing of cell death.

The findings demonstrated that in normal cells, psi healing specifically enhances the activity of those protein kinase groups involved in maintaining healthy cell metabolism, resulting in more rapid cell growth and cell multiplication, and accelerated recovery from disease and injury. Conversely, in cancer cells, negative psi intention specifically inhibits those same protein kinase groups so that cell growth and cell division slows down, the rate of programmed cell death is accelerated, and the tumours disappear. Psi healing has also been found to increase significantly the number of white blood cells that locate and kill cancer cells, known as cytotoxic (cell killing) T-cells, and to inhibit the production of a protein covering the cell membrane of cancer cells, that acts as a bio shield against immune cell attack. These studies have now been conducted successfully across a range of cancers. Psi healing also reduces the activity of protein kinase groups involved in the production of inflammatory cytokines (cytokines are small proteins produced by cells that serve as molecular messengers between cells) where unwanted inflammation was slowing down tissue healing.

Sean Harribance

While working at the MD Anderson Cancer Centre with Dr Lorenzo Cohen, a psycho neuroimmunology researcher, the noted healer Sean Harribance has achieved particularly successful results by inhibiting the growth of human and mouse cancer cells in Petri dishes, and, like Dr Bengston, curing cancers in mice after cancer cell injection. It was found that he stimulated a particular protein kinase pathway that accelerated cancer cell death.

A completely unexpected observation was how the mice responded when he came to their cage at whatever time of day. As soon as they saw him they would crowd together in front of him as if they knew he would heal them. Initially this was thought to be a chance observation, but the behaviour of the mice was consistent. Dr Cohen was so intrigued with this repeated observation that he got one of his staff, who had a very similar build and appearance to Harribance, to go to their cage instead. But on each occasion the mice took no notice of him. This response was similar to that of the mice in the Bengston studies who crowded to the left side of their cage.

Note: Sean Harribance (born 1939) has been involved in psi research throughout his professional life, and founded the Sean Harribance Institute for Parapsychology Research to further scientific investigation. He was the subject of a second University of Texas MD Anderson Cancer Centre study entitled "Human Biofield Therapy Modulates Tumor Microenvironment and Cancer Stemness in Mouse Cancer Carcinoma". This study demonstrated accelerated tumour cell death, increased anti-tumour immunity, and decreased cancer stem cell activity. A scientific study under the heading of "Empirical examinations of the reported abilities of a psychic claimant: A review of experiments and explorations of Sean Harribance" by Brian Williams that fully confirmed his psi abilities can be found in *Evidence for Psi: Thirteen Empirical Research Reports* (2015) by Broderick and Goertzel.

A meta-analysis

These non-placebo findings have received strong support from a meta-analysis of published empirical studies using psi healers (Roe, Sonnex and Roxburgh (2015). They found what is known as a 'significant effect size' (an estimate of the effect that an agent under test has on the target system compared with untreated controls) when psi healing was directed at encouraging seed germination, rate of seedling growth, proliferation of cells in vitro and rate of skin healing compared with controls. If the effect of psi healing in humans is nothing more than placebo effect, in the sense of being psychologically induced symptom relief as in pain reduction, then there should have been no difference between those seeds, cells and tissues exposed to psi healing, and those acting as non-exposed controls.

Discussion

The consistently positive findings from these non-placebo studies, in particular the Bengston studies with mouse cancer, and Dr Jains' review of the effects of psi healing at cellular level, strongly imply that the symptom relief reported by healees, both when receiving psi healing and afterwards, could be due to a healing effect occurring at tissue and cellular level as well as any placebo effect. This could lead to a reduction of inflammation, an enhancement of immune responses, accelerated tissue healing and inhibition of cancer cell metabolism. It could also slow down, or even inhibit the pathological changes occurring in chronic conditions. At present no mainstream clinical studies have been done to test this hypothesis, as the findings and implications of these non-placebo studies have not yet been recognised, so they have not been incorporated into medical thinking.

As editors of mainstream science and medical journals usually refuse to publish the findings of research using healers, the empirical literature on non-placebo studies is almost unknown in the medical world as it is published in non-medical, peer reviewed journals. Consultants and GPs have difficulty keeping abreast of their own specialties, let alone having the time to read outside their specialties.

Despite this, healers do form part of the complementary therapy team in some NHS hospital oncology units and in many hospices but, as noted before, as the findings from non-placebo studies remain largely unknown, any symptom relief is classed as placebo response only. In consequence, there has been no apparent reason to perform studies to see whether psi healing has a direct effect on disease pathology at cellular level. If, based upon the non-placebo studies, pilot studies were done, and the findings were positive for at least some pathologies, then for those conditions, psi healing would become classified as a medical treatment. The evidence from these non-placebo trials, including Bengston's finding, implies that psi healing can exert a direct healing effect at tissue level, as there seems to be no alternative explanation. This possibility may also help to account for the sustained, six-month symptom relief reported by many IBS/IBD patients following their 5 weeks of psi healing and may well have continued after that.

The case of Donald Clark also offers support for the possibility that psi healing can, and does, work at tissue level. He had accepted his consultant oncologist's prognosis of an inevitable continuing spread of his late stage lung cancer and probable death within about eight months. This nocebo effect (opposite to placebo as having a negative belief effect) was further reinforced by his consultant's referral to a hospice. He had no faith in healing, and attended only to satisfy his daughter's wish that they should try everything. It is, of course, possible that against all the odds this was a case of an as yet unexplained 'spontaneous remission' despite his despairing acceptance that his cancer was now terminal. But based on the findings from non-placebo studies, it seems more likely that he happened to receive healing from a particularly effective psi healer whose healing worked at cellular level, having a negative effect on the cancer cells that resulted in cure, as well as mental relief.

Scientific Evidence for the Power of Psi Healing

The nature of mind

These non-placebo findings, especially the Bengston and Sean Harribance findings, carry considerable implication concerning the nature and properties of mind. The everyday state of mind does not appear to possess the ability to affect anything other than the brain, but plays an essential role in receiving the placebo effect which, through the brain, can result in beneficial physiological changes. When those working as psi healers 'leave' their everyday state and 'enter' the psi state of mind then, while in that state of mind, there is considerable empirical evidence to show that healers can affect the metabolic activity of other living systems at cellular level. This, as noted earlier, implies that the mentality of the psi state possesses properties absent from the everyday state. The fact that we do not know how this is even possible does not alter the empirical fact of a consistent correlation between being in this state of mind and non-placebo results. This correlation implies that the psi mind must possess such properties. This was demonstrated by accident in the Bengston's trial when mice being 'healed' by embarrassed, self-conscious, biology students died, but survived when those same students entered the relaxed, psi healing mindset, when healing privately in their rooms.

At present we have no explanation beyond the concept of 'healing energy' or tentative theories of an extended bioinformation energy field through which a psi healer can sense and respond to the needs of the person, or animal, receiving healing. Margrit Coates (2001, 2003) presents many case histories of animal recovery from illness and injury, as well as cancer, after receiving psi healing that was very unlikely according to veterinary prognosis. These non-placebo findings are clinically important, and need to be taken seriously by mainstream medicine, with pilot studies done to assess whether psi healing has had direct effect at tissue level compared with controls. From the patient's point of view, any symptom relief, whatever the reason, is more than welcome.

2

EEG STUDIES REVEAL THAT THE BRAINWAVES OF HEALERS AND PATIENTS UNITE DURING HEALING

This chapter reviews the pioneering research carried out by the English researcher Cecil Maxwell Cade into the relationship between the mind of the healer and the mind of the healee during a successful healing session. Using Electroencephalogram (EEG) recordings of brain wave frequency patterns generated by healers during psi healing, and comparing them with healee brainwave frequency patterns while receiving healing, he made an astonishing discovery.

Maxwell Cade

Maxwell Cade (1918-85) was a physicist who had been a medical student at Guy's hospital, London, before changing course and qualifying in clinical psychology at Birkbeck

College, London. During WW2 he joined the Royal Air Force (RAF) to help develop improved radio navigation techniques and then transferred to the Royal Naval Scientific Service to work on marine radar. After the war he worked at the Admiralty's research centre at Harlow, Essex, publishing a series of research papers on infra-red radiation physics, clinical thermography and radar. He was elected a Fellow of the Royal Society of Medicine, the Institute of Biology, and the Institute of Electronic and Radio Engineers respectively, and was a member of the International Society for Clinical and Experimental Hypnosis. In 1963 he joined the Society for Psychical Research (SPR), became a member of Council in 1969 and was honorary secretary from 1973 to 1975.

His father was a staff officer in the Colonial Civil Service, and, thanks to the people he met through his father's colonial contacts, Maxwell Cade gained a profound knowledge of Eastern philosophy, including yoga and zen, and became an experienced meditator.[2]

His research programme

Cade's personal research goal was to provide a scientific basis for the study and practice of higher states of consciousness by correlating brainwave activity with different states of consciousness. In 1973, two wealthy Americans who shared his interests purchased a four-storey house in Chase Farm, North London, and financed the opening in April, 1974 of the Franklin School of Contemporary Studies, that ran day and evening classes on topics across the humanities. The school later moved to new accommodation in Chesterfield

---

[2] See www.mindmirroreeg.com/w/MaxwellCade.htm for full biography.

Gardens, Hampstead. Assisted by his wife, Isabel, Cade was Head of School, and developed a research programme correlating levels of consciousness with EEG brainwave profiles. Working in close collaboration with Dr Ann Woolley-Hart, a researcher into the medical applications of biofeedback at St. Bartholomew's Hospital, London, he used biofeedback as a method of enhancing the ability to enter higher states of consciousness. Cade died in 1984 following an abdominal operation and the Franklin School closed soon afterwards, bringing this exciting and innovative research in the UK to an end. It has been estimated that during the ten years of its existence some 3000 students attended Cade's courses and participated in his research. A noted student was Anne Wise, who returned to America to continue Cade's EEG research (Wise, 2004).

Cade's research findings

A key element of Cade's research programme was measuring and recording the amplitudes of the different brainwave frequencies known to correspond with different states of mind. Since their discovery by the psychiatrist Hans Berger in 1929, brainwave frequencies have been divided into four main frequency bands that have been shown to correlate with subjective states (1Hz equals 1 cycle per second):

Beta (13-40 Hz) – associated with normal waking brain activity.
Alpha (8-13Hz) – associated with passive, meditative mental activity.
Theta (4-8Hz) – associated with a dreamy state of mind.
Delta (1-4Hz) – associated with deep sleep.

Modern research since Cade's time has discovered that the brain can operate at frequencies up to 200Hz, banded as gamma and hypergamma, associated with very high levels of mental activity such as problem solving and creativity.

Cade teamed up with electronics engineer Geoffrey Blundell (1923 -2005) who, in the 1940s, helped to develop the cavity magnetron used by RAF Bomber Command during bombing raids in their radar target location system. Working together they developed an EEG brainwave recording unit called the Mind Mirror (figure 1).

Figure 1. The Mind Mirror Unit

The Mind Mirror consisted of 24 rows of light emitting diodes (LEDs) arranged in two banks of twelve rows each. The right bank recorded frequencies and frequency amplitudes from the right hemisphere and the left bank recorded the same from the left hemisphere. Twelve brain frequency steps were selected from the 40Hz to 1.5 Hz frequency range, with each row of sixteen LEDs responding to their designated brain frequency. These LED rows acted as sideways visual bars, lighting along differing lengths according to the voltage amplitude of their particular frequency as generated by the right and left hemispheres respectively. This created a bilateral visual LED outline profile of each frequency amplitude, rather like a Christmas tree, across the range of frequencies that correlated with reported mental activity. Later development involved projecting these profiles onto attached monitor screens. The present Mind Mirror 7 is now fully digitised.

Mind Mirror findings

Cade found that in everyday consciousness a person's bilateral frequency and amplitude EEG profiles flickered endlessly back and forth along their length as thoughts and feelings come and go, with no frequency relationship between the cerebral hemispheres. When students underwent training in meditative techniques he found that their EEG profiles became more stable, and their hemispheric frequencies tended to mirror each other as if the two hemispheres were working increasingly in concert. Cade was able to correlate these EEG profiles with reports of a participant's mental state. For example, when a person was in a steady healing mindset their frequency amplitude profile stabilised in the alpha/theta border around of 7.8 Hz (figure 2). A person in deep meditation showed a very similar profile centred around the alpha 8-9 Hz range.

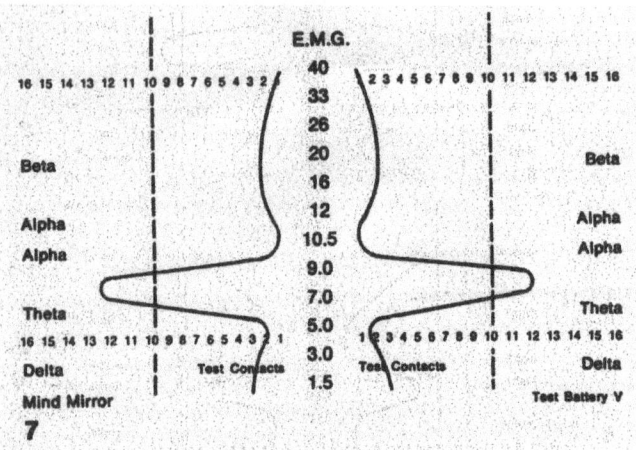

Figure 2. Typical psi healer EEG profile

These profiles varied slightly around a mean, but remained recognizably consistent for that person. Basing his findings upon Eastern meditative philosophy, Cade classified levels, or states, of consciousness into a descriptive hierarchy. Level 8 was the highest level, described by meditators as being in a state of cosmic consciousness. Deep meditation and the psi healing mindset were centred in what he termed Level 5, or the Fifth state, defined as being in a "Very lucid state of consciousness. Deeply satisfying. Intense alertness, calmness and detachment." (Figure 2).

Healer/healee EEG correlation

While Cade kept hundreds of careful notes and wrote many study modules, he died before writing up his research findings for academic publication. However, chapter eight of his book (Cade & Coxhead, 1979) is based upon his research notes, and the following is a summary of his findings as described in that chapter. Some well-known healers of the time who became involved in this research over several years were Major Bruce MacManaway, who makes frequent reference to Cade's research in his own healing practice (MacManaway & Turcan 1983), Edgar Chase, a retired physicist and his wife Hilda, Mrs Rose Gladden, and Lady Adeline Raeburn (wife of Major General Sir Digby Raeburn, then Governor of the Tower of London and Chair of the Institute for Complementary Medicine).

Cade's findings imply that when a healer is truly in the psi healing mindset their EEG profile shows a characteristic, bilateral maximum amplitude frequency at around 7.8Hz (figure 2) with associated smaller alpha amplitudes in the 16-20Hz frequency range and at a delta frequency of around 3Hz. He referred to this profile as the fifth state triad that correlated consistently with healers entering the healer mindset. He observed that during a successful healing session as reported by the healee, the EEG profile of the healee changed to closely mirror the psi healer's profile, as if the healee's brain waves had somehow become entrained by the steady brain waves of the healer. Before and after the healing session, healer and healee brain wave profiles were completely dissimilar.

On entering the healing mindset

When watching the Mind Mirror profiles of healer Mrs Raeburn, Cade saw that the differing frequencies of her right and left hemispheres slowed down and came into a typical psi healing profile over some 4-5 minutes as she left her everyday state of mind and entered the psi healing mindset ('psi healing' being my term not Cade's). Over a similar period with a slight lag the Mind Mirror profile of her relaxed client, initially completely dissimilar, settled into a similar profile and held it throughout the healing session. Afterwards they diverged back to completely dissimilar patterns. In Mrs Raeburn's case it was found that this joint entrainment was more pronounced if she laid her hands on the client's head rather than over, or on the site of bodily injury or chronic discomfort.

As an example, when giving healing to a policeman over several weeks who had suffered severe leg injuries following a car bomb explosion, little change in his EEG profile occurred while her hands were placed on his painful and stiff leg and improvement was slow. He still had poor balance on that leg and cycling was painful. When Cade suggested that Raeburn keep her hands on his head throughout the session, the policeman initially resisted the idea, blocking her healing energy as he said that the healing made him feel 'fuzzy', and as a policeman he must remain alert at all times. Eventually, when he agreed and became mentally relaxed, his EEG profile came into line with her profile for some 25 minutes, accompanied by a decrease in pain and an increase in rate of injury healing. Within three days he found that he could balance on this leg, there was an increased range of joint movement, and he could cycle without discomfort.

This initial observation regarding the effect of hand placement on healee profile was followed up with other healers. In many cases when using hands-on healing the healing effect was felt by the client to be more successful and the healee's profile came into closer entrainment when the healer's hands remained placed on the head of the client rather than the affected area. However, this was variable and very much depended upon the client's ability to mentally relax and trustingly 'let go'. It also depended upon whether the client was more receptive to receiving healing if the hands of the healer were over the affected area than over their head. As with the policeman the healer needed to explain very carefully what was involved to allay any subconscious anxiety of being 'taken over' by someone else.

In a series of experiments undertaken with Major Bruce MacManaway (who found his gift for healing during WW2 with injured soldiers) it was found that if a healer was standing behind the healee with hands on their head after they had entered into the healer/healee profile, the voltage amplitude of the profile increased incrementally as each of up to seven healers quietly joined the team with their hands on each other's shoulders. This implied an incremental gain of 'healing power' coincident with an increasing number of healers.

Distant healing entrainment

In an experiment to see if a healee's profile could be affected by distant healing, Edgar Chase, as healer, went into one room with Geoffrey Blundell acting as observer, and was duly connected up to the Mind Mirror. The healee to be, also connected to the Mind Mirror, remained in the consulting room with Mrs Chase. She pretended to be getting ready to do the healing, but would not be the actual healer. Cade and his wife, Isobel, stayed in the consulting room watching the healee's Mind Mirror patterns. Unknown to the client an arrangement had been made that when a clock struck the hour Chase would commence healing. On the stroke of the hour Chase's EEG came into the steady healing profile over the next couple of minutes, and the healee's EEG was observed to come into a closely similar profile with a 15-30 second lag. Both sets of profiles remained steady throughout the 10-minute healing session after which they diverged into dissimilar everyday patterns again.

A public demonstration

A striking example of healer-to-healee EEG entrainment across space occurred during the Wrekin Trust's Sixth Annual Health and Healing Conference, held at Loughborough University, UK in 1977 with an audience of 400 doctors, psychologists, scientists, healers and other professionals watching Mind Mirror monitors. On the stage Rose Gladden, an experienced healer used to travelling with Cade on such public demonstrations, was connected to a Mind Mirror monitor. Nora Forbes, wife of Dr Alex Forbes, then a hospital consultant from Plymouth who was present with her, volunteered to act as the healee, and was duly connected to a Mind Mirror monitor. The entire audience was able to observe Mrs Gladden's EEG profile change from everyday flickering through different frequency profiles to more sustained profiles as she passed through deepening levels of meditative calm until it settled into the profile of the healing mindset. Within a few minutes she was producing very strong alpha waves at around 7.8Hz as in Figure 2. Mrs Forbes' initially flickering EEG profile was observed to become more stable until it closely synchronised with Mrs Gladden's profile over the ensuing 15-minute-long session of healing.

As Cade remarked later, "It was such a clear-cut and undeniable demonstration, in terms understandable and convincing to all, that the audience was stunned. People cried; one or two even sobbed." (On a personal note I have met several healers who were there and said that the atmosphere was absolutely electric as they watched Mrs Forbe's profile coming into synchrony with Mrs Gladden's profile). In describing what she was experiencing during the healing session Mrs Gladden said, "I tuned into a large golden cloud and channelled this love through my heart and head to Nora." Mrs Forbes, who had initially felt rather apprehensive as to what she might experience, said that she had become deeply relaxed and refreshed during the healing. Mrs Gladden also said that she sensed there was something wrong with Mrs Forbes on her left side below her ribs. This was confirmed by Mrs Forbes who had been diagnosed with a problem to do with her left kidney.

The follow up

After the conference Dr Forbes approached Cade to say that he often felt frustrated at his medical inability to help certain patients further, and asked to be attached to the Mind Mirror to see whether he had any healing ability that could augment medical treatment. After watching for several minutes Cade found that his flickering profiles of mental activity were, as he put it, those of an 'ordinary academic' mainly beta. Before he decided to break the news that his profile gave no indication that he was a healer, Cade asked Dr Forbes to visualise a particular patient for whom he could do little by way of ordinary medicine. He then asked him to try to mentally heal this patient by sheer compassion. Almost immediately his dissimilar hemispheric brain waves began to slow down and, as the mental image of his patient stabilised, his EEG settled into the bilateral profile of a strong healer. Later, Dr Forbes was one of the founders of the Bristol Cancer Help Centre, now the Penny Brohn Cancer Help Centre, that opened in 1983 and employs a range of complementary therapies under medical guidance that includes healing.

Healing and healer health

According to Cade the Mind Mirror profile showed very clearly that if a healer was physically unwell, even if it was 'just a cold', and/or was feeling worried or run down, his or her healing effectiveness diminished. An ill, tired or stressed healer needed to take a break. For example, during a series of weekly studies with Mrs Raeburn, Cade observed a gradual falling off in the strength of her EEG profile, associated with a weakening of the pattern induced in the patient. She agreed that she was feeling rather tired and run down as she had many social and family commitments. After she had taken a holiday and returned refreshed, her healing power and healee response were back to normal. Cade observed this weakening of the healer profile with several healers during periods of reduced health and clients, unaware of the situation, corroborated this weakening of healing effect by saying that they didn't feel that they were getting as much benefit from the healing sessions. Cade proposed that the benefits experienced by healees may be explained by assuming that when brain and mind were in the induced fifth state during the healing session it augmented the body's natural healing processes, and the term 'neurohealing' has been given to this concept.

Swami Prakashanand Saraswati

As news of Cade's research spread, many eastern gurus, zen masters and swamis expressed an interest and visited the Franklin School to engage in his research. In 1976 Swami Prakashanand Saraswati, a noted master of meditation with some thirty years of practice, was touring Britain and attended the school for two weeks. His EEG profile demonstrated that he was able to maintain the fifth state with unwavering stability for hours on end even, on one occasion, when engaged in deep conversation with Professor John Hasted, then Head of Experimental Physics at Birkbeck College. As demonstrated by the Mind Mirror he was the most powerful healer who ever attended the school. When he went round the students and put his hands on their heads their Mind Mirror profile immediately entered into the fifth state. Saraswati, who had developed a system of meditation that he felt was applicable to Western students, had made a training tape that included chanting. When meditators, and most non-meditators, listened to the tape their Mind Mirror profiles progressively stabilised into the fifth state of meditation.

Identifying potential healers

Cade decided to use the Mind Mirror as a tool to discover if those who could attain and hold the fifth state depth of meditation were also potential healers. Over several months he tested one hundred students who had been trained to enter fifth state consciousness by including them acting in a healer-healee relationship with a healee who actually requiring healing. Of these students he found fifteen who were able to induce the healer/healee profile with reported benefits to the health of the healee. This strongly implied that to become a healer requires something more than just being in the meditative fifth state. He found that a potential ability to heal is not the same as becoming an effective healer. Many people may possess such a potential ability, but are ineffective through faulty technique, lack of understanding, lack of the necessary empathy for other people, and mind wandering during the sessions.

He therefore initiated an Introductory Course for Healers, covering elementary anatomy and physiology, together with practical instruction in mental preparation and healing technique, reinforced through EEG biofeedback. The course culminated in the award of a Certificate of Healing Competence based upon the ability to entrain the healer/healee profile as demonstrated by the Mind Mirror. His intention was to work with UK healing organisations and trainers to raise the general standard of healing effectiveness with resultant public and professional recognition. The National Federation of Spiritual Healers (now The Healing Trust), the World Federation of Healers and the College of Psychic Studies helped to fund his research and enable Cade with his Mind Mirror monitors to demonstrate healing at various conferences. After his death this initiative died away as none of the healing organisation had members with the requisite knowledge to continue his work or the facilities necessary to support it.

Ervin Lazslo

In Appendix 2 of his 2003 book *The Connectivity Hypothesis*, the philosopher of science and system theorist Dr Ervin Lazslo, described what he saw when attending two study seminars held in June and October, 2001, at the Institute for Communication and Brain Research, Stuttgart. On each occasion he observed the Hungarian psychologist, Dr Mari Sagi who, like Cade's healers, could induce healer/healee profiles as shown on monitor screens with reported improvement in symptoms. In her 2021 book *Remote Healing*, Sagi has published an account of her 30 years of research as a healer.

EEG Studies

Further Healer/Healee EEG Research

Further research since Maxwell Cade's time, using both EEG and fMRI (functional Magnetic Resonance Imaging) have fully confirmed his healer/healee EEG profile findings. (see Achterberg *et al.* 2005. Hendricks, Bengston & Gunkleman, 2010, and Bengston, 2017, 2019. The latter two papers can be downloaded for free from Bengston's website[1]). A review of the wider, post war, literature on EEG research using active sender/quiet receiver pairs of participants can be found in Charman (2006 a,b,c).[2]

3

STATISTICS SHOW LOCAL CRIME WAVES FALL DURING PERIODS OF GROUP TRANSCENDENTAL MEDITATION

This chapter is devoted to examining the evidence for the astonishing claim that when a group of people are in a form of meditation called Transcendental Meditation (TM), they can exert a calming and positive influence on the surrounding population. Based upon consistent sociological evidence this claim was made by Mahesh Prased Varma (1918-2008), known throughout the world as the Maharishi Yogi.

Transcendental Meditation

The practice of Transcendental Meditation™ is based upon the Vedic philosophy of a primal Universal Field of Pure Consciousness of which we are all part, and in which we are all immersed. The quantum physicist John Hagelin (1987) has proposed that this Universal Consciousness Field is the primary field, or ultimate fifth field, that underlies and unites the four force fields of physics (These are Gravity, Electromagnetism, the Strong Force that binds subatomic quarks together to form the neutrons and protons that comprise the mass of the atomic nucleus, and the Weak Nuclear Force involved in radioactive decay).

Practitioners of TM claim that when they are in a state of deep meditative unity with the Universal Field of Pure Consciousness their meditation can, and does, exert a beneficial influence upon the general mood and outlook of the surrounding population (for an updated account of TM theory, practice and social research see the Orme-Johnson website). They claim that this has been demonstrated by reductions in official crime statistics coincident with periods of group meditation. Mainstream sociology, in agreement with mainstream science and psychology, has not accepted these findings on the basis that whatever the subjective state of mind of one person or group of people may be, it cannot in principle affect anyone outside of themselves. Therefore, the apparent relationship is coincidence at best.

The Birth of TM

Mahesh Prasad Varma (1918-2008), the founder of Transcendental Meditation, was born into the high-status Hindu Kayastha caste. In 1942 Varma qualified with a degree in mathematics and physics from Allahabad University in Uttar Pradesh, one of India's top universities. This introduction to physics and mathematics would prove to be of seminal importance, as it enabled him to approach the psychological and sociological implications of deep meditation in a spirit of scientific inquiry.

LOCAL CRIME WAVES FALL

After qualifying, aged 24, he was engaged as an administrative secretary by Swami Brahmananda Saraswati who was the revered Shankaracharya (head monk and spiritual leader) of the ancient Jyotir Math monastery in northern India. Alongside his administrative duties Varma studied Vedic philosophy, giving many lectures and devoting himself to meditation. He became Saraswati's 'favoured pupil' and constant companion until Saraswati's death in 1953. As Varma, unlike Saraswati, was not of the Brahmin caste, he could not be named as his successor. Instead, he had been charged by Saraswati to devote his life to travelling and teaching Vedic philosophy and spiritual meditation to the whole world.

Before setting out on this mission Varma undertook a period of further instruction and meditation in the Himalayan town of Uttarkashi, a spiritual centre with many ashrams and temples, to become fully practised in a particular form of deep meditation that he termed Transcendental Meditation or TM. In 1955, aged 37, he left Uttarkashi and began lecturing and teaching TM, gaining the honorific title of Maharishi ('Great Sage') and Yogi (advanced spiritual meditator). During a huge mass meeting in Madras in 1957 he said that he intended to spread the teaching of TM across the world, and in 1959 commenced his first world tour that included America and, in the following years, Britain and Europe. With his academic background he was keen to encourage research into TM and over the years he established numerous teaching centres, colleges and universities, adapting TM to the needs of different social groups such as students, administrators, scientists and business people.

As is well known he influenced many prominent personalities including the Beatles. His basic message was that the greater the number of TM meditators throughout the world, the greater the harmony between individuals, religions, races and nations. During 1976 the Maharishi used his study of the yogic sage Patanjali's exposition of Indian yoga sutras, or mantras, written about 400 BCE (see Shearer 1982), to select the repetitive sounds of certain sutras as mantras to deepen the effectiveness of TM, and it is this method, known as the TM-Sidhi technique ('sidhi' meaning spiritual fulfilment) that is now taught by TM teachers.

The TM research programme

In 1973 the Maharishi International University (MIU) was established at Fairfield, Iowa, and Robert Keith Wallace, a neurophysiologist, was appointed as its first university president. In 1995 the MIU was renamed the Maharishi University of Management (MUM). Of particular importance has been the research led by Wallace into the neural correlates of changes in consciousness as reported by TM practitioners, and research by David Orme-Johnson and colleagues on the social influence of group TM practice.

Neurophysiological research

Electroencephalograph (EEG) recordings of the brainwave frequencies generated by the brain before, during, and after the practice of TM and later of TM-Sidhi, have demonstrated that in everyday life the complex patterns of impulse frequencies that spread across the cerebral cortex of each of the two hemispheres are normally quite different from the other, as each hemisphere performs its own set of functions. As the quiet, meditative state of TM, especially in the form of TM-Sidhi, is entered, and subjects report increased absorption into what they feel is a state of pure consciousness, their EEGs show that the frequencies of the two hemispheres come into increasing concordance with each other. This is known as interhemispheric frequency coherence. Parallel research explored claims of the beneficial effects of TM on psychological and physical health and reported reduction of illness and disease (Wallace,1986,1993).

Sociological research in TM: A radically new approach

As the number of people practicing TM increased during the 1960s, the Maharishi was receiving an increasing number of reports that organisations which included staff trained in TM experienced a more positive and creative environment with far less interpersonal friction. At the time meditation was considered to be a practice of personal spiritual enlightenment that did not directly affect anyone else, so one reason for this increase in social harmony might be that as their TM members were more peaceful and less confrontational at work, general stress levels were lower. In the western world meditation was, and is, practised by individuals in the hope that it will improve physical health, relieve mental stress, and enhance the body's self-healing systems. It has been the subject of much research into its mental, neurophysiological, general physiological and possible clinical effects. For a meta-analysis of published studies see Goyal *et al.* (2014).

With his science background the Maharishi interpreted these reports very differently. Because TM is based upon the Vedic philosophy of a Universal Consciousness Field in which we are all immersed, and because its practitioners feel that they come into direct union with this field during TM, he wondered whether the practice of TM was exerting a beneficial influence upon the general mood of TM co-workers who were unaware that some of their colleagues were practising TM. Could other minds, unaware of the existence of TM meditators in their midst, experience a calming effect in their everyday lives that would induce a happier and more positive state of mind?

During a 1974 TM conference the Maharishi proposed that on the basis of these reports, and the average percentage of TM meditators to overall organisational staff numbers, it was possible that as few as 1% of TM practitioners within a given population could induce beneficial social effects. To test this theory it was decided that the most practical indicators of any such change would be the official crime statistics for a given area. If the incidence of each type of recorded crime were reduced in an area where there were 1% or more TM practitioners, compared with comparable areas with fewer or no practitioners, this would support the hypothesis.

Pilot studies

Based upon this proposal a pilot study was carried out by Borland & Landrith (1974) using information from local TM groups in the USA as to the number of known practitioners in their area. They identified eleven small cities with 1% or more TM practitioners, and eleven small cities with very few to no practitioners. The official annual crime rates between the two groups of cities for 1972 and 1973 were then compared. It was found that in the non-TM cities the overall 1972/73 crime rates climbed by an overall 8.2% along with the national average, whereas in the 1% TM cities there was an overall 8.3% decrease in crime rates (Aron & Aron, 1986, pp.33-34). The probability that this difference was due to chance was estimated at a thousand to one against.

This implied a definite causal link between the presence of 1% or more TM practitioners, who practised twice daily 20-minute periods of meditation around the same time morning and afternoon, and the decrease in crime figures.

Dillbeck *et al.* (1981) revisited this pilot study by re-evaluating the comparative crime statistics, looking for all possible alternative social, economic and unusual weather factors over several years that might explain the difference. They then combined them with a new study comparing longitudinal crime statistics in another eleven non-TM cities, and eleven 1% plus TM cities, with comparable results. It was concluded that the one consistent variable appeared to be the continued local presence of 1% or more TM practitioners, whose overlapping, twice daily, periods of meditation resulted in a calming influence on the local population.

The unintended 1978 Rhode Island experiment

The State of Rhode Island and Providence Plantations, New England, on the east coast of the USA is a small, self-contained, densely populated state with Providence as its capital. In 1978 it had a population of around 750,000. By 1978 all TM teachers were now practising the TM-Sidhi technique, as EEG cerebral coherence studies had found that this technique resulted in a greater coherence, and an associated state of much deeper meditation, than the original TM method. Based upon the results of the Borland and Landrith study, this new experiment was set for the three month summer period of June through to mid-September 1978. Accommodation was booked in downtown Providence and the idea was that overlapping TM-Sidhi teachers would spend their summer vacation there, and offer Rhode Island residents the opportunity to learn TM-Sidhi so that when they left there would be at least 1% of residents continuing to meditate. Once this target was achieved, pre and post TM-Sidhi annual crime rates for Rhode Island could then be compared at a later date. Against all hopeful expectation, they found that the overwhelming majority of Rhode Island residents that summer were uninterested in learning anything about TM-Sidhi, so it was just the 350 or so of overlapping visiting TM-Siddhi teachers that sustained a continuous period of group meditation during that summer period. This was only about half of the 1% TM practitioners hoped for, but it was decided to go ahead with a revised study to see what social effects, if any, they may have had during the summer months of the project.

The results

Following the 3-month period of TM-Sidhi intervention, Rhode Island crime statistics for each of the summer periods from 1973 through to 1978 were collected and then compared. Across nine official categories of crime from homicides to car thefts the summer incidence for 1978 was down significantly. Traffic fatalities fell from an expected average of 34 to 14. The murder rate was 50% down and the burglary rate was down by 6%, resulting in 300 fewer incidents than expected. Stealing, from handbags in shops and restaurants to car thefts, was down by some 11%. In another social parameter the suicide rate dropped by 48%, the divorce rate was down and marriage rate up. These initial findings were collated by Zimmerman (1979) in an unpublished report and then re-examined by Dillbeck *et al.* (1986) using more sophisticated statistical techniques to correct for any overlooked chance variable such as exceptional summer weather, changes in employment opportunities, or changes in social policy. None were found, and Zimmerman's findings were confirmed.

The Maharishi Effect

So effective was the period of sustained group TM-Sidhi in reducing Rhode Island crime rates during the summer of 1979, that the Maharishi proposed that instead of a 1% presence of TM-Sidhi meditators in a local population as originally envisaged, maybe only the square root of 1% was needed to influence a defined population. This meant, for example, that while for a population of nine million some ninety thousand TM practitioners would be required at the original 1% level, only some 300 TM-Siddhi practitioners would be needed. This became known as the 'Maharishi Effect' or the 'Extended Maharishi Effect'.

After the Rhode Island experiment group TM-Sidhi interventions in cities in Holland, New Delhi and Puerto Rico were undertaken, and in each case a significant reduction in crime statistics was claimed (Aron & Aron, 1986, pp,113-120). Fifty-one studies at town, city, national and international levels, including war torn Israel and Lebanon in 1983 were completed (Aron & Aron, 1986, pp.121-127). In each case a lower incidence of death and injury from crime or a reduction in conflict intensity was found coincident with the period of group TM-Sidhi intervention.

To discover whether people were actually feeling any difference in their personal attitude to life, standardised quality of life survey questionnaires were carried out before, during, and after each period of TM-Sidhi intervention, and the consistent finding was an increase in positive subjective indicators that was sustained during the TM period, and slowly died away over the following weeks. The general mood in the population during the TM period was one of feeling more relaxed, more optimistic, and more friendly.

According to the findings of this research programme any improvement in crime reduction that occurred during the period of group TM-Sidhi intervention was not maintained but slowly reverted to pre-intervention norms after the meditators had left. To test this observation of temporary effect Aron and Aron (1981) carried out a study in Atlanta in which a small group of TM-Sidhi meditators were randomly assigned to different high crime areas at different periods of the year. In each case they found a statistically significant reduction in crime and antisocial behaviour in that district during the period of TM-Sidhi intervention compared with other years, followed by a slow return to pre-TM-Sidhi norms.

Mainstream sociological response

Despite the fact that well qualified researchers such as David Orme-Johnson, Robert Keith Wallace, Garland Landrith, Michael Dillbeck, Ken Cavanaugh, Herbert Benson, Candace Borland, Audrey Lanford and William van de Berg, had replicated these findings and had their papers published in peer reviewed journals, their findings and interpretation of TM effect have not been accepted by mainstream sociology. They have been accused of cherry-picking the data to support a ridiculous field of consciousness theory (Schrodt, 1990), or even if their findings of reduced crime rates were accepted as valid and coincident with periods of group TM-Sidhi meditation, they were dismissed as chance correlation because, as the claimed causal relationship was not possible in principle, it could not have occurred in practice.

The Arons quote one criminologist as saying that "The paper was beyond fault in terms of research design. It was impeccable. But I don't believe it. There is no explanation in current scientific thought that would explain this phenomenon." (Aron & Aron, 1986, pp.12-13). It seems that rejection of the research findings was, and presumably still is, based upon consensual agreement that neither individual nor group states of mind can possibly affect the mind of any other person or persons across space. The causal correlation inferred between the presence of 1% TM meditators, or the square root of 1% TM-Sidhi meditators in a community, and a corresponding reduction in crime statistics, could not possibly be true.

Orme-Johnson & Oates (2009) have summarised the arguments advanced for rejection of these findings and have mounted a detailed statistical reply to their critics. Deshpande & Kowall (2017, p.798) have argued that the statistical findings across all of these studies are valid and support the TM interpretation, saying that "In 1993, the Maharishi Effect was put to the test under the careful scrutiny of a distinguished review board in Washington, DC. The maximum decrease in violent crimes was found to be 23.3%. The statistical probability that this result could reflect chance variation in crime levels was less than 2 in 1 billion ($p < .000000002$).[3]

Experimental evidence for the spatial influence of group TM-Siddhi practice

While the Vedic theory of an extended consciousness field is considered by its supporters as being confirmed by these coincident changes in official crime statistics, the question remained as to whether evidence could be obtained to show that TM-Sidhi could exert a measurable effect at a distance. Orme-Johnson *et al.* (1982) designed an experiment that would operate during the period when some 2,500 TM-Siddhi practitioners, who meditated together at the same time for twenty minutes twice daily, met during a six week conference period from the 9th July to the 20th of August, 1979 in Amherst, a university and college town west of Boston, Massachusetts.

They recorded the EEGs of three meditators, two female and one male, each sitting alone in an electromagnetically shielded laboratory room at MIU, Fairfield, Iowa, some 1,170 miles (1883 km) inland west from Amherst. The three meditators, who were unaware of the purpose of the experiment, first meditated for an hour to establish individual EEG baseline levels of interhemispheric frequency coherence profiles as a neural marker of the depth of meditation. These three frequency profiles were then compared to see whether there was any degree of frequency coherence between the three meditators. They were then scheduled to meditate for periods that partly overlapped the periods of group Amherst meditation (some 80 sessions) whose times were known only to the researchers. After the Amherst conference was over a further set of comparative baseline EEG recordings were recorded during periods of meditation for six consecutive days in September.

Results

During all the EEG baseline sessions when the Amherst conference was not in group meditation each MIU meditator demonstrated a reasonably consistent level of personal interhemispheric coherence, but with minimal interpersonal brainwave synchrony with the other two meditators. During the sessions when part of their meditation period overlapped with an Amherst meditation period, their interpersonal frequency came into much closer synchrony as if they were responding to a common field frequency effect. The implication of this repeated finding during each of the 80 meditative overlaps with Amherst is that the three meditators were being influenced by the 2,500 Amherst meditators through the consciousness field. This finding carried the implication that the three MIU meditators fell into group frequency coherence during each session of Amherst meditation. This group frequency coherence was propagated through the hypothesised consciousness field, influencing the three meditators who were in a heightened state of meditative sensitivity.

The Amherst Effect

To test this claim of TM-Sidhi social effect, Davis and Alexander (1986), working in the Department of Psychology and Social Relations, Harvard University, collated crime, accident and suicide statistics for the whole of the USA for the summers of 1973 through to 1978, and then for 1980 and 1981, for comparison with the summer of 1979. They found a marked national reduction of incidence across all the crime parameters for the summer of 1979 during the period of the Amherst conference. This reduction applied to the USA mainland but not to the mid pacific islands of Hawaii nor to Alaska lying north of Canada. These two American states, at some 4650 miles (7483 km) and 3130 miles (5037km) respectively from Amherst, lay beyond the estimated 2200 mile (3540 km) radius of TM effect from Amherst's 2700 TM practitioners near the east coast of the USA. Canadian crime figures for the population living within the Amherst radius compared with other years were not collected.

Group TM-Sidhi brainwave synchrony and related studies

The possibility of group brainwave synchrony during group meditation is supported by philosopher of science and systems theorist Dr Ervin Laszlo. He describes observing a group meditation experiment during which the EEGs of twelve meditators were first out of step with each other, and then came into close brainwave synchrony of 81.2% for the twelve, and 98% for eleven, when the EEG of one meditator who remained partly out of synchronisation was excluded (Lazslo, 1996, pp, 109-110, figure 5D). What Lazslo had observed was one of a series of EEG studies carried out during group meditation by the University of Milan neurophysiologist Nitamo Montecucco (2000) with similar EEG synchrony findings across the series. As described in Chapter Two, Maxwell Cade reported similar EEG findings during group meditation as well as healer/healee brainwave correlation during a healing session.

That a similar level of deep meditation would be correlated with a similar profile of personal, interhemispheric brainwave frequencies, could be predicted by orthodox neuroscience theory. What could not be predicted from orthodox neuroscience theory, that states that each person remains separate and entire unto themselves, was that each individual, initially with out-of-step brainwave profile, would come into step with each other as if entrained into a common beat, with a main amplitude frequency of around 7.8 Hz. An analogy is soldiers on the parade ground, who are first walking at the same pace but in their own time, and being called to order and march in step.

Implications of societal TM effect

Whether the Vedic theory of a Unified Field of Pure Consciousness, upon which the working hypothesis of TM social effect was formulated, is valid remains unproven. What does seem to be well proven is that group TM-Sidhi (and presumably other meditative practices) does have a beneficial social effect. It falls under the heading of Distant Mental Interactions with Living Systems (DMILS).

These findings have not, to date, influenced mainstream scientific opinion that we cannot mentally affect anyone, or anything, outside of ourself. As presented in Chapter One, this mainstream position has been decisively challenged by a wide range of non-placebo studies using psi healers. In these studies the living system exposed to psi healing demonstrated a positive effect size response compared with non-exposed controls, and, in the case of mice injected with otherwise terminal cancer cells, near 100% cure.

The TM-Sidhi and psi healer state of mind

The intent of psi healers is to act as a conduit for the transmission of 'healing energy' into the healees to augment, or reactivate, the healee's natural healing systems of body and mind to achieve the highest holistic good. This holistic goal is not to be achieved through consciously willing the human healee or animal to feel better or be cured. Instead, the healer enters into a calm, disengaged state of mind, separate from everyday concerns, in which, as they express it, they 'stand aside' to allow the 'healing energy' to flow through them in response to the physical and mental needs of the healee. Similarly, TM-Sidhi meditators are not trying to influence the mental state of the surrounding population by a conscious act of will. The intent of each meditator, whether alone or in a group, is to disengage themselves from the everyday state of mind so that they can enter into a state of pure consciousness. Both sets of practitioners appear to enter into a similar psi state of mind, and, if the correct conclusion has been drawn from the comparative crime figures, group meditation happens to influence the unaware minds of others to beneficial effect as an unwilled consequence.

Is there a mental field?

As already mentioned, the TM explanation for the claimed societal effects of group TM Sidhi is that we are immersed in a universal consciousness field that acts as a carrier of mental affect when a person is in a state of pure consciousness. According to this claim, as in the Aron and Aron (1981) Atlanta study of local effect, and the Davis and Anderson (1986) study of the Amherst effect, the larger the group the greater the extent of calming social influence, as if there was group augmentation of causal effect across space. This implies that the hypothesised mental field acts as a vector field, with intensity of TM Sidhi influence slowly declining with spatial distance, rather than being of the same intensity throughout its extent as in a scalar field. Assuming a consciousness field exists, what is needed is a re-evaluation of the crime statistics to see if the percentage incidence of crime reduction falls away with increasing distance from the TM Sidhi source (vector field) or remains a constant to its limits of influence (scalar field).

Comment

The first two chapters have presented research findings consistent with the hypothesis that when practitioners of psi healing have entered the psi state of mind they can affect other living systems, both physiologically as in the non-placebo studies, and mentally. Sociological research has shown that when practitioners of TM-Siddhi are in a state of deep meditation, they are able to exert a beneficial mental effect across space that can be measured objectively by a reduction in crime statistics for the same period. Until someone can convincingly demonstrate otherwise, these are factual findings, and the fact that, as yet, we have no explanatory theory, is not a good reason to deny that these effects occur.[4]

4

VERIFIED OUT-OF-BODY OBSERVATIONS

The majority of clairvoyant experiences, during which people know what is happening elsewhere, occur when people are in a wide awake, psi state of mind in everyday surroundings as, for example, when Major McCoy was dowsing for the whereabouts of Meg's stolen harp, and when Dr Mayer's four intuitives were doing a reading for her (see Chapter 8). Such a clairvoyant experience seems impossible enough in itself, but at least it can be argued that it must have something to do with the mental properties of an awake mind when operating in a certain mode.

What really does seem impossible is when people say that they have been fully awake and observing a scene, including what people were doing, as if looking down from above when, in fact, they have been lying unconscious with eyes shut. When, for example, they have been in cardiac arrest while medical staff are trying to resuscitate them, or lying anaesthetised and unconscious with eyes taped shut and their face covered with a surgical drape while undergoing surgery, or being kept sedated and unconscious to give their brains time to heal. In other cases, such a clairvoyant experience has occurred when someone has fainted after receiving an overwhelming emotional shock, or have been knocked unconscious by an accident. The common factor in all these cases is that whatever the cause, they are unconscious, and, in many cases, unresponsive even to painful stimuli.

Out-of-Body Experiences

These observations have occurred during what are known as Out-of-Body Experiences (OBEs), because that is how they are remembered by the experient on recovering normal consciousness. As far as they are concerned they know, with absolute certainty and great clarity, that they really were 'up there' floating near the ceiling while looking down at their inert body and observing what was going on around it, or even leaving their room and seeing what was happening elsewhere.

From Dr Raymond Moody's groundbreaking book *Life After Life* (1995) onwards, thousands of such out-of-body observations (OBOs) occurring during OBE experiences have been published in dozens of books and hundreds of articles. They are usually included alongside the now very familiar accounts of near-death experiences (NDEs), in which those who have experienced a NDE are convinced that they have seen a prevision of eternal life to come. They remember in vivid detail features such as leaving the body, passing through a dark tunnel towards the Light, meeting deceased friends and relatives, seeing beautiful surroundings, hearing glorious singing or meeting a religious figure and then, in many cases, being told to go back because it's not their time (see Moody, 1975, Fenwick & Fenwick, 1995, Parnia, 2005, 2013, Sartori, 2008, 2014, van Lommel, 2010, Rivas, Dirwen & Smit, 2016).

Unlike a NDE in the now familiar 'I left this world and went to heaven but had to return' scenario, an OBO relates to what is happening in the here-and-now of this life, so it is potentially verifiable by those who were observed to be present at the time. The following nine accounts, adapted and in some cases extended, have been taken from *The Self Does Not Die: Verified Paranormal Phenomena from Near-Death-Experiences* (2016) by Titus Rivas, Anny Dirven and Rudolf Smit. Their excellent and fully referenced book includes dozens of cases of NDEs considered by them as evidence of life after death, but my interest in this book is restricted to those OBO accounts that have been checked and fully verified by those in a position to do so. (The case and page number as given). The famous Pam Reynolds case, and the Man with the Dentures case have not been included as full details can be found in their book and online. The nine cases are as follows:

1. A surgeon "flapping" his wings (Case 1.5.pp. 9-12)

In the late 1990s Al Sullivan, a New England van driver, was experiencing worrying heart arrhythmias. Hospital tests showed that one of his coronary arteries was completely blocked, requiring immediate heart surgery. While the operation was being performed under sustained anaesthesia, Sullivan's eyes were taped shut and his head was covered by a sterile drape. On his recovery he told Dr LaSala, his cardiologist, about his NDE during which he had seen deceased loved ones in a glorious yellow light. As he listened LaSala assumed that what Sullivan had probably experienced was a hallucination caused by his drugs, and in consequence, would probably have thought no more about it. But Sullivan then went on to describe what he saw during an OBE, when he felt wide awake, and as he listened LaSala realised that something very different had happened for which he had no explanation.

Sullivan said that he was looking down into the operating theatre from somewhere near the ceiling, and saw his body lying flat on the operating table covered with light blue sheets. He could see that his chest had been cut and held open to expose his chest cavity and saw his heart. At the same time he saw his surgeon, Mr Hiroyoshi Takata, standing close by "flapping" his arms with his elbows bent, looking as if he was trying to fly. He also saw two surgeons working on one of his legs, which puzzled him, as he did not know at the time that part of a leg vein would be used to replace the blocked coronary artery.

LaSala realised that what Sullivan had seen, despite being flat on his back, anaesthetised, his eyes taped shut and a drape over his head, was technically quite correct.

After donning his sterile operating gown, Mr Takata always guarded his sterile hands by keeping them flat against his chest and indicating what he wanted done by vigorously pointing with his elbows. This was not something that any of the other surgeons did. Sullivan said that when he saw Mr Takata flapping his arms he was standing on his own near Sullivan's newly opened chest cavity while the other two surgeons were removing a length of vein from one of his legs. All of Sullivan's observations were confirmed by the surgical and nursing staff present, as well as by Mr Takata who, during a video re-enactment, said, "I cannot explain how he saw these things under the complete sleep of anaesthesia." Later, in a filmed Japanese interview in 2009, Mr Takata said, "Frankly, I don't know how this case can be accounted for. But since this really happened, I have to accept it as a fact. I think we should always be humble to accept the fact. I think science has not yet sufficiently revealed the ability of human beings. There exists in this world something that cannot be captured by science and mathematics."

2. *The cigarette smoking grannies (Case 2.14. p.44)*

In 1994, 17-year-old Michaela of Homer City, Pennsylvania, was travelling on summer vacation with her family when their car was hit by a truck. While other members of the family were shocked, but suffered relatively minor injuries, Michaela suffered a serious brain injury plus injuries to both arms, and went into a life-threatening coma during her helicopter transport to hospital and ICU. Her coma lasted a fortnight, and, at some time during that fortnight, she had a NDE in which she saw her past and future. She also had an OBE that she described to her mother as soon as she could after recovering consciousness.

During her OBE she first found herself up in a corner of her room looking down at her body on the bed. She then left her room and saw her parents sitting in the hospital cafeteria with her two grandmothers who were sitting together opposite them. Then, to her complete astonishment, as she said in an interview:

> My dad is a smoker and he said he was gonna have a cigarette because he just wanted to have some breathing room and get out of there. And it was funny because my grandmother, my mom's mom, who would never, has never, and would never, have a cigarette in her life, was like "Oh, I need one too. I'm gonna have one too." And then my other grandma was like "Yeah, me too."

Michaela's mother confirmed that this had happened on a specific day during one of their visits to the hospital. She remembered it because she was just as astonished when, completely out of character, her own mother was feeling so stressed that for the first time in her life, she decided to have a cigarette, and then her mother-in-law decided to have one as well.

3. The red headed nurse who ignored him (Case 2.16. pp.46-47)

Don (pseudonym) had been involved in a terrible traffic accident, suffering multiple limb fractures, bruised lungs, severe heart bruising and a head injury. Rushed to ICU in Appleton, Wisconsin, his limbs were immobilised in suspended traction to stabilise the fractures in alignment, and his neck was immobilised in a neck brace. He was catheterised, placed on artificial ventilation, and kept unconscious under sedation for many days to allow his condition to stabilise.

During this strapped up, immobilised, and unconscious period, he had a very unusual OBE. He was telling a nurse with red hair, who was doing routine nursing checks and administering his medication, that he badly needed to go to the bathroom. She just ignored him and left the room. Feeling totally frustrated at her bad manners he decided to get out of bed and follow her to give her a piece of his mind. He walked out of the ward through glass sliding doors, then followed the sound of voices round the corridor corner before seeing a group of nurses sitting at a central station chatting and working on computers. He again saw the nurse, now on a computer, walked up to her, tapped her on the shoulder and started to talk to her, but she still completely ignored him. Feeling really irate, he leaned against the counter, crossed his arms and stared at her, thinking "I'm going to stay right here until she notices me." She still ignored him, so, feeling thoroughly exasperated, he eventually gave up, stomped back to bed, and fell asleep.

Dr Bellg, his ICU doctor, now takes up the story in her 2015 book *Near Death in the ICU: Stories from patients near death and why we should listen to them*. A fortnight later with his complex bone fractures now stabilised and head injury improving, Don was weaned off sedation and his ventilator and respiratory vent removed. Still furious with the nurse, he couldn't wait to tell them about her, saying that he wanted to make a complaint. They knew what night his OBE must have happened, as this nurse was a visiting nurse who had been finishing her two month shift in the hospital, and had checked him that night before ending her shift and moving on to another city.

His description of going through sliding glass doors along a corridor and round a corner to get to the central nurse station was correct, as was his detailed description of the layout of the central station, including its computers, the ice machine, blanket warmer, supply cart, and where the nurse with short, wavy, red hair was sitting. But she had left that ICU a full fortnight before he was awakened from sedation and his artificial ventilation removed. At the time, he was immobilised and unconscious, so he could not have seen her, and certainly could not have got out of bed to follow her. He could not have seen the glass doors, the bend in the corridor, and details of the central nursing station layout including where she had been sitting. It seems that the start of his OBE coincided with this nurse's attending him while doing routine checks, and a feeling of urinary urgency, maybe caused by the indwelling catheter.

Despite Dr Bellg's gently suggesting to him that, given his circumstances at the time, he must have had an OBE, Don looked at her in complete disbelief. He had great difficulty in accepting this explanation as his experience had been so real, and remained so vivid in his mind, that it must have happened in real life. It could not have been some imaginary so-called OBE. Realising that it might take some time for Don to accept what had happened, Dr Bellg calmed him by saying that she'd had a word with the nurse manager and he could register a complaint if he wanted to. But this satisfied him, and he did not mention the subject again.

4. The nurse training centre (Case 3.33. pp. 112-113)

Another of Dr Bellg's patients was Howard, a chronic alcoholic who, after an extensive abdominal operation, had suffered a cardiac arrest that required repeated defibrillation. After five days on a ventilator he had recovered enough to be weaned off it. As soon as his breathing vent had been removed he told Dr Bellg and a nurse about his unusually extended OBE in which he had seen and heard what they were all doing during his resuscitation. He had watched as Dr Bellg inserted a "hose" into his throat and heard her say that the mucus in his throat was "very sticky and is really fighting me". He also saw, as Dr Bellg confirmed, that she was wearing the same vivid, lime green, blouse that he could see in the 'V' of her white coat the day she resuscitated him. Where his OBE observations markedly differ from others is what else he saw. Early in his OBE he felt himself shoot out of his head and up towards the ceiling of the ICU. Then, in his own words:

> I felt myself rising up through the ceiling and it was like I was going through the structure of the building. I could feel the different densities of passing through insulation. I saw wiring and some pipes and then I was up in this other room. It looked like a hospital

ward but it was different. [...] It was very quiet and it seemed like no one was there. There were individual rooms all around the edge, and on some of the beds were these people, except they were not people, exactly. They looked like mannequins and they had IVs hooked up to them but they didn't look real. In the center was an open area that looked like a collection of work stations with computers.

What he didn't know was that up on the next floor, right above the ICU, was a nurse training centre, arranged exactly as he described, in which new nurses practised their techniques on the mannequins in the separate rooms that simulated ward rooms before being admitted onto the wards.

After looking round the strange room he went back down through the ceiling into his body. He then "floated" out again, saw electrodes on his chest, heard someone (Dr Bellg) say "Turn up the juice" then "Okay, charge". Then, after Dr Bellg said "Everybody clear" he saw his body suddenly arch upwards from the bed and his NDE ended.

5. The 12-digit number (Case 2.5. pp. 35-36)

Professor Norma Bowe, College of Education, Kean University, New Jersey, recounted this case in a 2012 Near Death Experience Network documentary called "Beyond the Light." At the time she was working as a nurse in ICU. An unconscious woman with a head wound had been admitted to the ICU and had remained in a coma for several weeks. During that time she had to be resuscitated after suffering a cardiac arrest. When she came out of her coma, had been unhooked from the respirator and her vent removed, she was able to talk again. She told nurse Bowe that she had

had an OBE and had seen her room as from above. Already familiar with such stories, Bowe was listening, but not taking much notice until the patient told her that she had an obsessive compulsion disorder about numbers. If she saw an isolated number she had to note it and memorise it. Once she had memorised it she never forgot it. As she was looking down during her OBE she had seen a 12-digit serial number stamped on the top of the tall respirator unit near her bed and had obsessively memorised it. This could not be seen by anyone standing alongside it. When the respirator was scheduled for removal a member of staff used a ladder to go up and dust the top. He was asked to read out the number stamped on the top, and it was the same 12-digit number, which the patient had seen during her OBE.

6. The 1985 quarter dollar coin (Case 2.6 . pp.36-37)

Ricardo, aged 82, suffered a cardiac arrest during dinner one evening and was admitted to the Texas Medical Center Hospice, The Medical Center, Houston, Texas. Dr Lerma, working as an intern at the time, was involved with his resuscitation that required administering an electric shock to restore his heart rhythm. On recovering consciousness Ricardo had just enough time to indistinctly murmur something about "seeing the light", and seeing something else before he suffered a second, more severe, cardiac arrest. This time an epinephrine injection direct into the heart was needed to restore its rhythm, and his heart eventually stabilised overnight.

During Dr Lerma's ward round next morning Ricardo waved him over, and insisted on telling him more about his NDE. After he had finished he then said that he wanted to confirm that his OBE had been real and not just some kind of hallucinatory dream. He told Dr Lerma that "When I was out of my body and floating above the trauma room I spotted a 1985 quarter lying on the right-hand corner of the 8 ft high cardiac monitor. It was lying amid the dust as if someone had put it there for this very reason. Dr Lerma, could you please check it for me? It would mean so much to know I had seen it".

To please him Dr Lerma found a ladder, and, in the presence of some nurses, climbed up to look. He later wrote, "To our total amazement, there it was, just as he had seen it, and even the year was right: 1985". As he remarked, Ricardo was in no position to climb up and put it there for himself, so the only way he could have seen it was when he was out of his body and high enough to look down on the dusty top of the cardiac monitor for himself.

7. His wife's red trouser suit (Case 2.7. p. 38)

This next case is an example of an OBE occurring when experiencing severe emotional distress and shock at what was about to be done. In 1978, retired British army major Derek Skull, then in his fifties, was admitted to intensive care following a major heart attack. Placed in a side ward room which had windows very high up, reaching to just under the ceiling, he had recovered consciousness, and had been lying there for the last two days still feeling very unwell. In 1995 Dr Peter Fenwick, neuropsychiatrist, and his wife Elizabeth Fenwick, MA (Cantab), consultant on health and family matters, met Derek, and in their 1995 book *The Truth in the Light: An Investigation into 300 Near-Death Experiences*, they recount what happened to him as told in his own words (pp. 34-36). After admitting that he was probably not the world's easiest patient he said:

I was lying there feeling terrible – absolutely at my lowest point, I'd never felt so low. Then these women just descended on me like three witches. They had to insert a catheter. I'd never had anything done like that and they gave me no warning; nothing. I didn't know what they were up to. I remember shouting "Who's that dreadful woman in the white coat?" and someone saying, "That's the doctor." I felt this enormous tension as though I knew something was going to happen. Then I felt absolutely airy-fairy – as if I was levitating, quite serene, withdrawn from my body. I floated up to the top left-hand corner of the room. I looked back and saw my own body lying there with its eyes closed. It didn't seem surprising for me to be up there. I could see through the windows at the top of the room to the reception area outside in the ward. Suddenly I was conscious of my wife waiting at the reception desk, talking to someone who was sitting down behind the desk so that I couldn't see them properly. She was wearing her red trouser suit. I thought 'My God! What an inappropriate time to arrive. It's not visiting hours. I haven't shaved, I'm looking dreadful, and anyway, I'm up here and she's down there, and there's the body. What's going to happen?'

The next thing I was conscious of was being back in my bed. I opened my eyes and sitting beside me was Joan in her red trouser suit. I wasn't a bit surprised because I knew she'd arrived. I'd already seen her.

Questioned by the Fenwicks the couple were asked if the red trouser suit had any special significance, but apparently not. Joan was a painter who was very aware of colour, and she had decided to wear the red suit as she felt that it was a cheerful vibrant colour and would cheer him up. He was surprised to see her at reception because, as he said, it was outside visiting hours and he was feeling truly dreadful. The reason why his wife was there is not included in the story, but because Derek was so obviously distressed at the idea of having a catheter inserted, the staff may have asked her to visit to calm him down. Some two years later the BBC ran a programme on OBEs and Major Skull recounted his experience.

8. *A straight line on the monitor (Case 2.8. p.39)*

Dan O'Dowd was 27 years old when, in 1979, he was hit head-on by a drunk driver on the Pacific Coast Highway, and over the next two years he required some 50 operations. During a 15-hour operation at the Cedars Sinai Medical Center, Beverley Hills he had an NDE, and was fully conscious as he felt himself rise out of his body. Looking down he saw a straight line on the monitor and heard the doctors saying they thought he was dead. He then left the operating room and went into a hallway where he saw his family being informed that the operation had failed. He then returned to the operating room to see the doctors still trying to defibrillate his heart. "One guy grabbed those big thumpers on me and someone put some gel on me, and I'm looking down and I look terribly dead. Then they put those big shockers and blast away. The first time nothing. The second time it started me back up, and immediately I could feel myself being sucked back under the anaesthesia. And out." Dan told the medical staff and family what he had seen and experienced, and his account was confirmed by both parties. In an article in the Los Angeles Times his surgeon Mohammed Atik, said that he had no medical explanation for what Mr O'Dowd's said he had seen during his OBE.

9. *Visiting home (Case 2.12. p.42)*

Dr Barbara Rommer, of Fort Lauderdale, Florida, happened to investigate this unusual case (Rommer, 2000) as Pat Meo, the wife of Tony, who was in a coma when the event occurred, was a nursing supervisor at the Holy Cross Hospital where they both worked and told her the story. Tony was undergoing open heart surgery in a hospital in Milwaukee, Wisconsin, some 1250 miles (2012 km) away, when he arrested for 30 minutes, and remained in a coma for the next 2 weeks. When he had recovered consciousness he told Pat that he had an OBE in which he had 'floated' back to their home, and saw that the person looking after their house was having sex with a girlfriend whom he described in detail. At the time, Pat had inwardly dismissed his account as no more than a hallucinatory dream until, to her surprise, the man confirmed what Tony had 'seen', including Tony's description of the girlfriend. But what really convinced Pat and Dr Rommer of the genuineness of his OBE was Tony's description of the mail strewn over their dining room table. He had seen a Danish office supply catalogue that had arrived unrequested in the post. Besides his OBE Tony also had a NDE vision of life after death, during which he had been told by a higher being that he was being sent back to bear witness to his NDE. This higher being also told him the date of his death. About a year after Tony had died, Pat found a small piece of paper in one of his desk drawers. Written on it was "Return date, August 29." The day that he died.

Discussion

In each of the nine cases someone has claimed to have observed something as if they were awake when, according to ongoing clinical monitoring, visual observation, and sensory tests, they were unconscious and their eyes were shut. The reason these claims cannot be dismissed as dreams, imagination, or hallucination is that what they said they had observed during their OBE was later verified by independent observers as occurring as described. So how can we seek to explain the phenomenon we call OBEs?

Two states of mind

In my previous book, and in the preceding chapters, I have proposed that the evidence for the existence of psi phenomena is sound, and lends support for the hypothesis that consciousness can operate in two different states of mind: the everyday state in which we are limited to incoming sensory information about the outside world, and act upon that world through bodily activity, and a psi state of mind that can mentally access information directly, as in telepathy, clairvoyance and precognition, act directly upon other living systems as in psi healing, and, in certain circumstances, affect physical objects across space (psychokinesis, or PK). A consistent feature across all OBEs is that, as far as it can be judged, they probably exist for only a few seconds to maybe a minute or so, in real time, but experienced as occurring for much longer. They seem to occur at some random moment during unconsciousness and, if occurring during resuscitation of a cardiac arrest, only once per arrest. The question is, how can OBEs be accounted for during periods that, as far as outside observers are concerned, including anaesthetists, a person is unconscious and certainly has their eyes shut.

A psi mind hypothesis

It is proposed that when brains are in this state of unconsciousness, the everyday state of mind, dependent on sensory input for awareness, is in abeyance as little or no sensory stimuli is coming in, so only the non-sensory psi mind is potentially available. For the psi mind to be activated to a state of conscious awareness, there needs to be a brief surge of brain activity sufficient to sustain an OBE, associated observations, and the laying down of memory for later recall. This seems to be in contradiction to the conditions in which OBEs are assumed to occur, which is one of complete unconsciousness, either natural, or under anaesthetic sedation. The question is whether momentary brain activity sufficient for consciousness is possible in such circumstances.

The dying rat brain experiment

Dr Jimo Borjigin, Associate Professor, Molecular & Integrative Physiology, Associate Professor, Neurology, University of Michigan Medical School, used rat brains to study what happens to a dying brain by monitoring electrical brain activity from the moment of cerebral blood loss following induced cardiac arrest to actual brain death (Borjigin *et al.* 2013). They inserted thin wire electrodes, connected to an electroencephalogram (EEG), into the brains of nine rats for highly sensitive direct contact recording of all brainwave activity from cortex to brainstem. They then induced cardiac arrest whereby the blood supply to the rat's brain suddenly ceased, and recorded what happened from the moment of no cerebral blood supply to the moment of irreversible brain death through final, deoxygenated, metabolic collapse. These findings were then compared to recordings of brainwave activity taken in conscious and anaesthetised rats.

What they found came as a complete surprise. It contradicted the assumption that from the moment of cessation of cerebral blood flow there was a rapid and uninterrupted decline in brain function to brain death. Shortly after suffering complete blood loss, each of the nine dying rat brains generated a roughly 30 second surge of intense, coherent, brainwave activity across all the frequency bands from low delta (1-3 Hz) to high gamma (70-150 Hz plus). In humans the latter is associated with high-level conscious functioning in humans. This surge of electrical activity that swept through the whole of each rat's brain before collapse into final flat-lining was described by Borjigin *et al.* as "highly coherent".

In her discussion of what she and her team consider to be the implications these findings concerning the occurrence of NDEs, Borjigin commented that "the data suggest that the mammalian brain has the potential for high levels of internal information processing during clinical death. The neural correlates of conscious brain activity identified in this investigation strongly parallel characteristics of human conscious information processing" (Borjigin *et al.*, 2013, p.14436). These findings indicate that for a brief period between clinical death and actual death the brain becomes momentarily as active, or more active, than in the normal waking state, generating neural correlates of high-level conscious processing. She concludes her discussion by saying:

> The NDE represents a biological paradox that challenges our understanding of the brain and has been advocated as evidence for life after death and for a non-corporeal basis of human consciousness, based on the unsupported belief that the brain cannot possibly be the source of highly vivid and

lucid conscious experiences during clinical death. By presenting evidence of highly organized brain activity and neurophysiologic features consistent with conscious processing at near-death, we now provide a scientific framework to begin to explain the highly lucid and realer-than-real mental experiences reported by near-death survivors (p. 14436).

Greyson, Kelly and Dunseath (2013) have challenged this implication on the grounds that the recorded bursts of EEG activity were smaller in amplitude compared with pre-death EEG activity and have not been paralleled by any EEG findings in dying human brains prior to resuscitation. This objection overlooks the EEG findings of Chawla, Akst, Junker, Jacobs, and Seneff (2009) who recorded a sudden surge in brain activity in seven patients just before death. Greyson *et al.* pointed out that in many cases of remembered NDEs, it seemed to last far longer than thirty seconds, but this is purely a subjective impression. While Greyson *et al.* found Borjigin *et al.*'s finding interesting, they dismissed them as relevant to the occurrence of NDEs and their implications that during the NDE the experient had seen what life would be like after brain death.

In response, Borjigin, Wang and Mashour (2013a) restated their finding of an increase in power and tight phase coupling across the full frequency range bands. This included an eightfold increase in high frequency gamma band activity normally associated with high level mental information processing. They proposed that their unexpected findings have clearly "demonstrated the presence of electrical fingerprints of consciousness in the near-death brain" and conclude that "in the light of this information we respectfully disagree with the opinion of Greyson and colleagues and strongly believe that our findings will contribute to a better understanding of near-death experiences". Borjigin's findings imply that NDEs are not an exception to the rule that for all mental activity there must be neural correlation. They do not occur when the brain is functionally moribund, but during a brief period of intense brain activity.

Implications for OBEs

It sems to me that Borjigin *et al.*'s findings indicate the likely neurological origin of NDEs and OBEs. It seems that a seemingly unconscious brain may spontaneously generate a short period of coherent brain activity which would not display any outward sign. If sufficiently intense for the generation of a vivid NDE, then it would certainly be sufficient for a brief observational period of an OBE. Looking up at our immediate surrounds, as when lying down, is not our usual viewing platform, and, when we do so, things look unfamiliar. We normally view our surroundings at about the same level or from above. It is proposed that in the cases described here, as well as thousands of other cases, the momentarily conscious psi mind experiences its clairvoyant awareness from a familiar viewing position, either looking down from above as in a panoramic view, or sometimes looking around at shoulder level, and presents this viewpoint to the everyday mind on re-awakening.

None of this explains how the psi mind 'sees' during an OBE, any more than we know how what we see 'out there', which is our immediate reality, is related to streams of optic nerve impulses occurring in the visual centres of the brain inside the darkness of the skull. The one factor common to everyday seeing and psi mind seeing as in OBEs is conscious awareness. When we understand the nature and properties of consciousness of itself, separate from experiencing ourselves as being conscious, we will have our answers.

5

Evidence That Personal Possessions can Mysteriously Disappear and Reappear, or Turn up Somewhere Else

We all mislay small items that we handle frequently like keys, tv remotes, wallets, and so on. Whatever the 'it' may be, say a key, it is not where we 'know' we put it because we 'always put it there'. We search 'everywhere' with increasing exasperation, give up, search again, then suddenly '*There* it is'. We then remember we'd gone there to unpack something we'd bought, and must have put the key down behind that without realising it. Search over, explanation complete, peace returns.

There is, however, another category of occurrences for which the range of normal explanations such as forgetfulness, or misplacement do not seem to apply. For example, the missing door key is suddenly back in its usual place days or weeks later, or is found somewhere else that doesn't make any sense. In the absence of an explanation its reappearance is eventually dismissed with an irritable shrug of the shoulders as 'just one of those things'. But what if it is more than that?

Quite independent of each other, two reputable investigators of paranormal phenomena, intrigued by such inexplicable experiences and impressed by the circumstantial evidence supporting these claims, decided to inquire further. One was Mary Rose Barrington (1926 to 2020), an accomplished cellist, who studied English at Oxford University, qualified in law, and pursued a legal career, first as a solicitor and then a barrister. With a lifelong interest in psychical research she was a member of the Society for Psychical Research, contributing many research papers and appointed Vice President. In her 2018 book *JOTT: When things disappear ... come back and relocate: and why it really happens*, she published the results of her investigation into 180 cases where the inexplicable had occurred, and coined the term 'Just One of Those Things'(JOTT) to refer to such cases (Barrington, 1991).

The other investigator is Dr Tony Jinks, Senior lecturer in Psychology, University of Western Sydney, Australia, and a consultant on the Australian Institute of Parapsychological Research Review Board. His 2018 book *Disappearing Object Phenomenon: An Investigation,* summarises his investigation into 385 cases of disappearing and reappearing objects that could not be accounted for by memory lapse, absent mindedness, inadequate searching, third party trickery, or deliberate deception.

Mary Rose Barrington

We will start with the findings from Barrington's cases, collected over many years of investigation. Like Jinks, each case was carefully checked against a list of possible explanations such as memory lapse, absent mindedness, inadequate searching, third party trickery, deliberate deception, and so on, to eliminate interpretive error. Of her 180 cases, Barrington presents 74 examples in her book, from which 16 are presented here.

When Barrington examined her cases of Jott she found that they could be grouped into six main categories. These categories are described below, with examples of each.

The first two categories are **Walkabout** when an article disappears from its known position and reappears somewhere else, and **Turn-up** when an article disappears from where, if memory is correct, the owner thinks it was before disappearing. Similar in consequence to walkabout but without knowing for certain where it was originally.

The gold locket

A woman had left her gold locket and chain on her desk overnight, but when she went to pick it up next morning it had disappeared, and despite carrying out a thorough search it remained missing. Then, she told Barrington, *some three years later* "my son took his washing out of the machine and, lo and behold, the locket and chain was on top of his clothes".

The hairbrush

A man took his usual hairbrush with him on a three week holiday to Kenya with his brother, but was unable to find it when packing his single suitcase for his return to the UK in January, 1976. Checking whether his brother had borrowed his hairbrush but not returned it, he searched his brother's suitcase as well, but it was not there. One day in September, nine months later, he walked into his bedroom to see it lying on the floor.

The white gold necklace and pendant

On January 12, 2006, an elderly couple said goodbye to their visitor, who returned a couple of minutes later to say she had just found an unfastened, delicate white gold necklace with a diamond studded pendant stretched out horizontally across the front path by the gate. The necklace did not belong to her hosts or to anyone they could think of who lived locally. The next day, their chiropodist, who had visited a week earlier, called again and they told her the story. In reply she said that she wished she could find her necklace which she had taken off, fastened, and placed on the arm of her sofa late one evening on either the 3rd or 4th January. When she went to pick it up she found that it had disappeared, and she still couldn't find it. To their mutual amazement, when the couple showed the necklace to her, it was her necklace as she had described it to them. During the 8/9 days between her necklace disappearing, and the departing visitor finding it lying horizontally across the front path by the gate, many visitors as well as the owners had walked up and down that same path in daylight when it would have been in plain view.

The square orange washing up bowl

Late one evening Mrs P was tidying the kitchen while her husband took the dogs for their usual walk. She had taken the square, orange, washing up bowl out of the sink and put it on the work-top. After she had finished other tasks she turned to put it back into the sink, only to find that it had disappeared. On his return they both searched the kitchen for it without success. She went to bed feeling, as she said to Barrington "a wee bit scared". Unable to find it despite renewed searching she bought a new, red bowl. A week or so later she decided to use her rarely used pressure cooker, kept in a rarely opened ground level cupboard normally blocked by a leg of the kitchen table. She moved the table, opened the door to get the pressure cooker out, and, having done so, she saw the orange washing up bowl in the space behind the pressure cooker. It was so tightly wedged in the back space that they had difficulty in getting it out, finding that it still contained some dirty water and a missing teaspoon.

The missing Dick Francis book

Before going to bed Mrs W, who was staying with her daughter's family, settled down to read a thriller by Dick Francis. After going to the bathroom she returned to find it had completely disappeared, and, despite later searching, remained missing. It was not found among the books her daughter packed when they moved house. Several years later in her own home when in search of some candles, Mrs W reached into the bag where she kept them alongside her Christmas ornaments, and out came the book.

Car keys inside a locked car

A woman drove to her office, and let herself in with the office door key that was on the same ring as her car key with which she had locked the car. When it was time to go home she could not find her key ring despite desperate searching. When she wandered over to the car, wondering how on earth she was going to get it home, she looked in and saw her bunch of keys on the car seat inside the locked car.

Bracelet on the stairs

Told to Barrington by 22-year-old LH who was living with her parents at the time.

"A bracelet my mother made for me vanished just a few months after it was given to me. Seeing as I hate losing stuff, I tore the house apart trying to find it. Eventually I gave up and moved on. Weeks had passed since I had lost it. Then one day I was going up to my room when I looked on the stairs, and my bracelet was sitting on a step, neatly curled up as if someone had put it there. The staircase had been vacuumed many times, so there is no way it could have been there all along".

The disappearing bathrobe

Miss M decided to have a shower, went into the bathroom, shut and *locked* the door. Hanging her bathrobe on the door hook as she always did, she proceeded to have her shower. After finishing she stepped out and reached to take her bathrobe off the hook, but it was not there. To her baffled astonishment she eventually found it lying at the foot of the stairs.

From the window sill to outside

This remarkable walkabout occurred in Mrs VS's house, Croydon, during the evening of April 12, 2000. The result

Evidence

was witnessed by herself, her close friend Mrs CW, who had contacted Barrington through the SPR, two neighbours, Barrington herself, and the police who came at Mrs VS's request.

The landing window consisted of a stout aluminium frame, with the left window fixed, and the right window hinged from the top to open outwards. It was held closed by two, stiff to turn, latches, that required turning to 90° to release the window which could then be opened by pushing at the bottom. Mrs VS is certain that it was closed when, earlier in the evening, she went past it to the bathroom before entering her bedroom, the door of which was directly opposite the landing window. After watching a television programme she came out of her bedroom at about 9.30 as she thought she had heard a noise earlier. She noticed that the window was now open to about six inches (150mm), so she checked the house, but there was no disturbance anywhere. The downstairs doors and windows were firmly locked as usual.

Returning to the landing she saw that a row of plastic pots containing plants and seedlings had vanished from the window sill but were not lying spilled on the carpet. When she looked out she saw the pots lined up in horizontal order on the 20° sloping glass roof of the conservatory some four foot below the landing window with no spillage. To be placed there by whatever agency would require turning both stiff latches 90°, opening the window, lifting the plant pots up and over the raised bottom rim of the aluminium frame, clearing the outside window ledge, and then lowering and placing them in a straight line onto the sloping glass roof without tipping any of them over.

The responsive coin

Raymond Bayliss, author and landscape painter tells this story:

> In 1957, during an afternoon, a friend and I, while walking on Hollywood Boulevard, stopped at a leather goods shop. While my friend was chatting to the owner, I spied a Canadian coin, a penny, on the desk and examined it. The coin was of a type I had not seen before, and on the reverse side it bore a scratch. I asked the store owner if I could buy the coin, but he said he preferred to keep it, and as my friend and I left the store I looked back at the coin wishing I could have bought it.
>
> After we had walked about a hundred feet away from the entrance to the store something touched my elbow and my pant leg. I immediately looked down at the sidewalk and saw the identical penny by my foot. Needless to say, I carefully examined the coin and saw that its reverse side bore the telltale scratch. My friend was as surprised to see the penny as was I. I can see no normal, mundane explanation for the incident. Obviously the store owner would have found his penny was missing and no doubt assumed that I had taken it. But viewing the entire incident it represented a disappearing object on one end, and a mysteriously appearing object at the other.

Diary in the long grass

In 1986 Miss VT, who kept a meticulous diary, wrote to her friend Dr John Beloff, former President of the SPR, to say that "2 weeks ago I couldn't find my diary, which lives here by my couch within reach, taken out to note an appointment etc., and immediately put back. I *never* carry it anywhere. I searched under the couch, behind and under the cushions etc. – nothing. I felt rather desperate as I really needed it.

Yesterday I washed a shirt, found the line downstairs already full of the lodger's washing, so had to go to the farther one from which one can see the back garden. I noticed a darkish something at the far end in the thick grass, and that was my diary, very wet. I *never* go there, nor does anyone else, unattended jungle."

The third category is **Come-back** when an article disappears from its usual, known, place and returns there again. Two examples are given below.

A new outfit

For a special occasion, Mrs M bought a new outfit, which she hung in her wardrobe. When the occasion arrived and she went to put the outfit on it had disappeared. Sometime later the family moved house, the wardrobe was dismantled by the removers and re-assembled by them in her bedroom in their new home. Later, when unpacking her clothes, she opened the expectedly empty wardrobe and saw the new outfit hanging on a rail. When she contacted the removers they assured her the wardrobe had been empty when they dismantled and when they re-assembled it.

The returning magazine

Mr C. carefully put down a magazine in a particular place, as he knew he would be wanting an article in it for reference a week later. When, a week later, he went to pick it up it was not there, and he and his wife searched for it in vain. Thinking that, however unlikely, he must have thrown it out without realising it, he left it at that. Some three months later, while tidying up the room, he found the magazine in the same place he had put it three months earlier.

The fourth category is **Flyaway** when an article disappears permanently without trace.

Here I must intrude a personal note. The following case concerns the late British psychologist Professor David Fontana, University of Wales, Cardiff, who had been President and Vice President of the Society for Psychical Research, author of many books, and a careful investigator of psi phenomena. Like Barrington I had the pleasure of knowing David who was, by nature, definitely not the sort of person who would haphazardly lose or misplace things. This is his account as given to Barrington.

The red leather folder

"I used to bank with Coutts, and even when I transferred to a local bank I kept all my Coutts bank statements in the very distinctive red leather folder, embossed with gold lettering, that never left my study. One day I opened it and went through the statements in order to find the date on which I had purchased some conifers to plant at the bottom of my garden. The matter was an important one, as my neighbour was claiming compensation for some alleged root damage caused by these trees, and my insurance company needed to know the date of planting in order to reject the claim.

After checking the date, I put the folder together with the statements on the table in my study and left the house for work. On my return I entered my study to write to the insurance company, and looked for the folder plus statements to check once more the date, but had an immediate and very odd premonition that I would not find them. They were not on the table, and although I literally checked every shelf, every drawer and every file in my study they were nowhere to be seen.

I then wondered if I could possibly have put them in my briefcase and absentmindedly taken them to work (very unlike me, especially in view of the importance of the documents concerned), but they were not there. I checked with my wife and our two university aged children to see if they had been in the study and picked up the folder, but with no results. The Coutts folder and statements were never seen again."

Luckily, his insurance company accepted the date that he remembered from the statement, and the claim never materialised.

The fallen paint brush

In the summer of 1957 RB, a professional artist, was teaching a student still life painting, working in an empty storeroom furnished with two stools and an easel. The room was brilliantly lit by the sun and the floor was covered wall to wall in brown linoleum. While illustrating a certain technique he dropped his paint brush, a special eleven inch long, one inch wide, long handled, black No 2 Delta brush, and they both heard it hit the floor. He immediately bent down to pick it up but couldn't find it despite the fact that it could not have rolled very far. They searched the floor, including under the two stools and easel, but the floor was empty and it was never seen again.

The four-inch cork stopper

This was personally reported to Barrington in April, 2011, by MM.

"Ten days ago I was cooking. I opened a stone jar which has a large cork stopper, some 4 inches (102 mm) in diameter, in which I keep dried porcini. I took out what I needed, put the porcini in a jug, poured on boiling water, and turned round to replace the stopper and put the jar back in its place. The stopper had gone, and it hasn't turned up despite an exhaustive search of our very small kitchen."

The fifth category is **Windfall** – when an article of unknown origin is found where it could not have been before: (maybe from someone else's *flyaway?*).

Gold finger ring on a cabinet top

In a letter to Barrington dated September 12, 1983, a woman recounted a jott experience that had occurred some 13 years earlier. Her husband had recently completed a 6ft high, built-in cabinet, that she had decided to dust one day while cleaning. She could just reach the top with her duster on tiptoe, and, as she swept the duster across the top, a gold ring fell to the floor. Neither she, nor her husband, nor her three young children had ever seen it before. As it happened to fit her finger she started to wear it. Feeling curious about it, as it was not a modern ring, she took it to a jeweller who said that it was a Victorian keeper ring that were very popular in mid Victorian and Edwardian times. They were prenuptial or betrothal rings, given a year before the official engagement as a symbol of the giver's intention to marry their intended bride. The final category is **Trade-in** when a known article disappears and is replaced by a similar article of unknown origin: (again, might it be someone else's *flyaway*).

EVIDENCE

The stoneless gold ring

On the morning of December 26, 1987, Mrs L was in the kitchen with her mother and K, her very young daughter, who was in her low chair resting on the floor. She took off her four finger rings and placed them on the worktop as usual before donning rubber gloves to wash up. After an hour, during which both she and her mother had often bent down to talk to her daughter, she went to put her rings back on but could find only find three of them, the missing one being a gold, single stone, dress ring. They searched the kitchen unit and surrounding floor without success until her mother, who had seen the four rings on the worktop, so confirming that they had been there, suddenly saw a glint on the floor and said, "Is that it by K's chair?" But, to their surprise, it wasn't her single stone dress ring, but a gold ring with a setting for three stones, all missing, that neither of them recognised; nor did her two sisters or her father. Despite further kitchen searches, including pulling the sink unit out, they never found her ring and could find no explanation for the stoneless gold ring.

A pair of unrecognised fish knives

Mr Brian Wisker, then senior partner of the estate agents, A.C. Frost & Co, told Barrington the following story. When his sister got married she received a set of twelve Elkington fish knives and forks which she cherished. One day, when she got them out of the drawer, she found only five pairs instead of six, and the missing pair were never seen again despite searching. Several months later, a fish knife and fork pair of the same high quality but not of the same design or make, appeared alongside the other five pairs. Neither his sister nor brother-in-law recognised them.

Barrington's hypothesis

The context

Barrington first makes the point that while the term 'anecdotal reportage' is often equated with 'unreliable' in scientific estimation, what is actually meant by 'anecdotal reportage' is eye witness testimony concerning a particular event, or series of events. History is built on eye witness testimony of events as contained in historical records. Criminal trials and jury verdicts depend upon legally tested anecdotal reportage, from a pathologist's report to eyewitnesses of an incident. Indeed, much scientific research starts from an anecdotal report accepted as a reliable observation of an unexpected experimental finding. The difference between the anecdotal reportage of scientific experiments and single anecdotal observations, is that scientists make repeated anecdotal observations, either personal observation of the phenomena under test, or of instrumental recordings, on those things in the universe that, by their very nature, are repeatable in controlled circumstances.

Barrington points out that whereas scientists expect acceptance and respect from their peers concerning their anecdotal observations, those who eventually pluck up enough courage to report the occurrence of a jott know that they are likely to be met by polite disbelief at best, and ridicule at worst. This being so, you can be sure that they have exhausted every relevant avenue of inquiry before being brave enough to say that a jott has occurred, as it goes against their own belief as to how the world works as well as the belief of others. In consequence, many people probably keep quiet as they don't wish to look foolish, dismissing the uncomfortable experience as 'just-one-of-those-things'. This implies that the actual incidence of jott experiences is probably very much higher than its reportage.

Barrington then places the occurrence of jott within the context of repeated observations by many people, including skilled investigators, of paranormal phenomena. These include cases of poltergeist stone throwing, raps, bumps and bangs, movement of objects, table turning, electrical interference, and so on, which should not have occurred in an orderly, cause and effect universe, but which have been observed to occur beyond reasonable doubt. Paranormal phenomena and instances of jott are paranormal in the sense of being physically acausal in incidence. If an event can be shown to be explicably causal as in A to B, then it is not paranormal. The same principle of causality, she says, applies to spontaneous telepathy, clairvoyance, presentiment, precognition, healers and healing. She quotes the positive findings of empirical research into telepathy, clairvoyance, precognition, and psychokinesis that support the claim that these anecdotal accounts of jotts are describing a real phenomenon.

The hypothesis

Barrington presents her hypothesis as to why a jott can happen in chapter five *Psi Reality: A Framework for JOTT*. She points out that the principle of probability of repeated occurrences is built into the universe, with the most likely occurrences, such as an apple falling down to the ground instead of falling up towards the sky, as having an almost infinite probability of occurrence. We term such probability of repeated occurrence as 'cause and effect'. But the improbable can occur as well, like outliers at either end of a probability Bell curve. Paranormal events are so improbable as to seem impossible by any causal explanation, but they do occur, and the one consistent feature they all seem to share is that they occur only in association with the human mind. This being so, Barrington proposes that a *human mind-acting-on-matter* relationship must exist. She dismisses the philosophical position of mind-brain dualism as she feels it cannot explain how matterless mind can affect matter as they are different in kind. Instead, Barrington proposes a form of monism in which the universe, including all living things, is composed of one kind of stuff that she calls *Mindstuff*. This can exist in two states: a 'matter state' consisting of particles, atoms, compounds, etc., existing in a state of physical actuality that we observe as objects in three-dimensional space; and a 'mind state' consisting of thoughts, feelings and desires concerning physical things such as our possessions as well as the wider world.

She proposes that the existence of a universal principle of probability at cause and effect level, and consequent evolution of the universe, implies the existence of a lawmaker, as in an all-embracing Cosmic Mind. That within the Cosmic Mind there exists a hierarchy of individual mind-states, including our human mind-state, that exist in some degree of autonomous dissociation from the Cosmic Mind. Jotts, and the whole range of paranormal phenomena, occur when our human mind-state interferes with the normal causality of the matter-state. Jotts happen when, for some unexplainable reason, our mental-state at some unaware level somehow interrupts the cause-and-effect matter-state on which an object, such as key, depends for its existence, to de-materialise in an unobserved moment of spatial discontinuity and disappear. Later, perhaps as the result of an unaware change of mindset, this effect disappears and the key re-materialises in an unobserved moment back into normal spatial continuity to be seen again, either where it was originally, or elsewhere, or sometimes as a flyaway key unrecognised by the baffled recipient. She proposed that paranormal physical phenomena can be considered as a momentary aberration of mental effect on matter which otherwise, for 99.999% of the time, interacts in a lawfully causal manner with the normal 'matter state' of brain, body, and the world around us including our personal possessions.

Dr Tony Jinks

By the time that he wrote his book Dr Jinks had investigated some 385 personal accounts from Australian and New Zealand sources of objects that have unexpectedly disappeared for good, re-appeared, appeared for the first time or been replaced by another similar object. While 'Disappearing Object Phenomenon' is the title of his book, Jinks also uses the term 'Just one of those things' or jott, as first coined by Barrington (1991), together with 'jottle' and 'jottling' when referring to their anomalous behaviour. Here are his two opening examples.

Kate

One evening in August, 2008, Kate drove home after work to her small suburban house situated in a quiet residential street. With her car key on the same ring as all her other keys she selected her front door key, and opened the door at the same moment that her telephone rang. Knowing who it would be, she left the porch door open inwards with the key still in the door, and dropped her bag to run down the hall to answer the phone. After the call she went back to take the ring of keys out of the door and pick up her bag. The bag was there on the mat untouched, but the ring of keys that she had left in the door lock was not. She searched and searched in vain, eventually concluding that, however improbable, someone must have entered the porch and snatched the keys in that brief moment of opportunity, although as far as she could see, the street was empty as usual and there was no one about. The next day, still unable to find them, she was faced with the inconvenient and very expensive business of getting a new car key cut as she had only the one, and engaging a locksmith to change the locks of her front door, back door, garage and mailbox plus getting a new key cut for her office. Within the year she moved to a new, permanent post in another city, and bought and renovated an apartment close to the city centre. One evening she returned home, placed her new set of keys in the hallway drawer as she usually did and went into her bedroom, only to see her old set of keys on her old key ring lying on her pillow. As she said to Dr Jinks, when she saw them she felt "nauseous and giddy" with shock. As no one else had a key, no one else could have entered her apartment in her absence and left them on the pillow.

Mark

One evening Mark, who is sitting on the sofa with his large, black, tv remote control on a cushion beside him, rashly decided to switch television channels while Courtney, his partner, was in the kitchen preparing a snack during an advertisement break. On her return she was less than pleased at his unwanted initiative, and he hurriedly reached for his remote to switch back, only to find it was not there. Assuming that it must have fallen between the sofa cushions or onto the floor they searched in vain, turning the sofa upside down, and even crawling round the floor on their hands and knees. Unable to find it Mark bought another one, but a few weeks later while Courtney was out seeing friends, he visited the bathroom and returned, only to find that this remote had also disappeared, and remained missing despite frantic searching. Later that week he bought another remote, but a few months later that disappeared overnight, leaving him completely baffled, as on this occasion he distinctly remembered putting it carefully back in its cradle next to the tv before going to bed. Feeling that enough was enough he decided to engage in the heathy, if inconvenient, exercise of getting up from the sofa to change channels and volume via the television controls.

Dr Jink's analysis of jott behaviour

After years of personal investigation into such claims, Jinks, like Barrington, decided that these accounts of unexpected, inconvenient, and definitely unwanted, object disappearances, reappearances, and so on, could not be attributed to forgetfulness, unaware misplacement, faulty memory, removal by someone else etc. What was being repeatedly, and independently, described was a genuine phenomenon.

Statistical analysis

Jinks submitted his 385 cases to a statistical analysis to see if he could identify any clues as to a possible common cause. He simplified Barrington's six types of jott into three: *disappearances* (including *flyaways*), *appearances* (including *turn-ups* and *windfalls*), and reappearances (including *comebacks* and *walkabouts*). This leaves the occasional *trade-in*, in which a known object disappears and is replaced by an unfamiliar one, as in Mrs L's stoneless ring, a kind of double jott, Here is an example of a trade-in as personally recounted to Jinks:

Deborah

A year or two ago I went to the library to borrow some books. I got out three or four, one of which was called *Foulshot*. I don't remember the others, but I'll always remember this book because of what happened next. I checked the books out at the counter and put them in my library bag. On the bus I looked at each of them, wondering which to read first. I know I put them all back when I closed my bag up. When I got home I emptied the bag on the table, and all the books were there except *Foulshot*. Instead, there was another book, I can't remember the author or title but it was a historical novel. This was not the book I looked at on the bus, although it was from the same library. Over the next week I read the other books except this one as it did not interest me. I took them all back a week later and put them into the return slot. I didn't investigate further. I never went back to the library to see if *Foulshot* was still on the shelves. Also, I never received any correspondence telling me that *Foulshot* hadn't been returned. I've never understood how one book could have been replaced by another book in my bag on the bus trip home.

Typical objects that jott

Like Barrington, Jinks found that the objects most frequently involved were jewellery items as in rings, brooches and necklaces; single food and beverage items; keys; small computer items such as USB sticks, computer 'mice' and television remote controls; grooming items such as combs, brushes, hair clips and tweezers; kitchen utensils such as knives and forks; wristwatches, wallets, credit/debit cards, individual coins, stationery, small tools, and items of clothing such as hats, gloves and scarves. Here's Michelle's account of her disappearing leggings.

Michelle

"I once threw a pair of leggings onto the bed and went back to the wardrobe to find something else that would go with them. I had my back to the bed for no more than a minute, but when I went to put my leggings on they were gone. No one had been in the room with me because I had closed the door, and would have heard if someone had come in. I looked everywhere but never found them again."

Jott activity

In order of Jott activity Jinks found that the most common behaviours were disappearance and later reappearance of that same object, often in the same place but sometimes elsewhere in the house. Then the unfamiliar appearance of a new object that could not be accounted for, or an unrecognised object replacement that was similar to the original but definitely not the original, and then disappearance for good. It is possible that the latter may have turned up somewhere else to be seen by the surprised recipient as a new object (a 'flyaway' from elsewhere?). Monetary value was not a particular factor in the frustration of loss by jott, but sentimental attachment certainly was, as Lucy's experience demonstrates.

Lucy

Lucy often wore an inexpensive, slightly oversized ring that was of considerable sentimental value. When she was busy in her bedroom one evening the ring slipped off her finger. She heard it hit the wooden floor, and bent down to pick it up but couldn't find it. She then undertook a thorough search, armed with a powerful lamp, and eventually called in the help of a friend to move the furniture, but without success. She then vacuumed the floor, hoping to suck it up, but again without success. Finally, she crawled round the floor with a large magnifying glass, but she never found it.

Chris

Sometimes a nondescript object of no interest, except in a practical sense, turns up somewhere completely unexpected as Chris found to his surprise. Chris's car was parked in his garage at home and locked as usual. He was the only person to use the car and no one else had the keys. One day, when he got into the car he saw a box of matches on top of the dashboard. They had not been there when he last drove the car into the garage, as they would have been too obvious to miss, and he didn't smoke in the car. He was also the meticulous sort of person who kept his car neat and clean. Although it didn't make any possible sense, he did wonder whether it was the matchbox normally kept in a bowl in the living room next to the cigarettes, but, as he was about to go out, he did not go back in to check, so where the match box came from remains unknown,

General findings

As a general rule, Jinks found that the sooner an object has been recently handled and then noted as missing the quicker it returned although, as Kate, Mark, and Michelle found, there were many exceptions. As for jott experients, most had just a single experience, but some were what Jinks termed as jott repeaters, with two or more over the years. Males and females seemed roughly equally affected, with women more likely to lose items of jewellery by jott, whereas men lost more electronic items. The great majority of jott experients were adults from their twenties onwards, and as far as Jinks could judge, as a class of people they were indistinguishable from non jott experients. Most had little, or no, prior knowledge or interest in parapsychology, had no idea that this experience had happened to anyone else, and remained baffled and often emotionally disturbed by their experience as it made no sense. Jinks found no significant difference in levels of education, types of career or occupation, or types of hobbies between those who have experienced a jott and those who have not.

Prevalence of jott phenomena

As for population prevalence of jott phenomena, like Barrington's 180 cases, Jink's 385 jott experiencers were obviously not random, but self-selecting in that they were so unable to find a normal explanation for their experience that they responded to public requests for such accounts. As part of a psychology study at Western University, 80 people volunteered to take part in an anonymous survey without knowing the purpose of the study. The survey included questions asking whether they had ever experienced an incident such as a 'strangely behaving object' and, if so, what was the nature of their experience. The result was completely unexpected. Jinks, like the researchers, had assumed that very few such cases, maybe two or three at most, would be reported. But 42 participants (52%) reported having had a jottling experience that they were unable to explain. If this finding was extrapolated to the general public, it implies that millions of people, may have experienced an unexplainable object disappearance, reappearance, first appearance or replacement, eventually dismissed in baffled distress and exasperation as 'just one of those things'. Whether the prevalence varies according to type of community, culture, or beliefs remains unknown.

Jott characteristics

As Jinks found, in agreement with Barrington, jott behaviour demonstrated several characteristics that applied to all of them. They were either 'there' or 'not there' in their entirety, and if they re-appeared they were exactly the same as when last seen. Objects were never seen to fade out of existence or fade back into existence. During absence their disappearance was total. If a key had a patch of rust, or was slightly bent before disappearance, then that is how it was on its re-appearance. In every case the jott object possessed the same physical properties as non-disappearing objects.

While jotts are never observed to disappear or appear because they are either there or not there, it is just possible that someone, as in Sophia's experience, may occasionally catch a fleeting glimpse of a returning jott in the act of rematerialising into our reality before seeing it in the normal way as their missing possession again.

Sophia

I had a very funny experience from a few years back that I still recall to this day. I have a silver bracelet with little leaves attached to it by small lengths of chain all around it. There are about 20 or so leaves and one day I noticed that one was missing. The chain links were there but with nothing on the end. I was upset, but didn't think any more of it as I assumed it had been pulled off the chain somehow. As it wasn't that noticeable I still wore the bracelet. Anyway, about a month or two later I was in my room at home, sort of staring into space thinking of something when I saw this small silver thing appear before my eyes in the middle of the room. It was there for about a second, then dropped to the floor. It was my missing leaf.

Jink's jott experiences

In his last chapter Jink explains that his interest in jott phenomena stems from his own experiences of disappearances and reappearances for which he could find no everyday explanation. It seems that, for no reason that he can discover, he is a 'jott repeater', and provides several examples from which I have chosen the following three accounts.

Despite suffering from a painful rib injury, Jinks was determined to play cricket the following weekend, and decided to practise during the week in preparation for the match. The problem was that he did not possess a bat as he always borrowed one from the team kit. Returning home at around 3:00pm that Saturday afternoon after watching his team play, he remembered that he had a 'junior bat' somewhere in the garage under loads of unsorted junk, but decided he couldn't be bothered to look for it right then. At 5:00pm he locked the house and with his family went to join friends for a meal, returning home by car at 9:00pm. Unlocking the door he was first in. When he switched on the lounge light he saw the 'junior bat' leaning against the bookcase. It was certainly not there when he went out, and he and his family had definitely not looked for it. This, he suggests, was an appearance jott occasioned by his intention to practise batting.

One Wednesday evening he noticed that his wallet was missing from where he usually put it in a drawer with his glasses and keys. Sometimes he put it on the kitchen counter, or the dresser, or in the front zip of his work bag, or beside the bed, but it was in none of these places and he searched the house in vain, both then, and during Thursday when he was working from home. Feeling very frustrated he cancelled his credit/debit cards, and on Friday drove into town to get a new driver's licence. Friday night is sports night for his boys, so as this can get rather tense he was in the habit of chewing gum to relieve parental stress. Reaching up into an overhead cupboard he took out some gum packets and had turned to clear up the kitchen counter when he heard his wife utter a gasp of surprise. She had opened the cupboard door a few seconds later to take some gum packets as well and there, on the shelf above the gum container, was his wallet. He could not have missed seeing it when he looked in for the gum packets because it was a large, fat, black leather wallet and the cupboard was white. It must have reappeared back into human observation in the few second interval between the two openings of the cupboard.

Early one Saturday morning he was repairing his front fence, intending to replace a section with new wire netting after first attaching strands of new strand wire between the posts, and had bought two new rolls of strand wire, now nearby on the ground, ready for use. He knew he also had a used half roll somewhere in the garage if he needed it, but had not bothered to look for it. During the task he stopped to chat to a neighbour, being only some ten steps away and in full view of the area to be re-fenced but not looking at it in particular. After they parted he turned round to find both the shiny new rolls and the somewhat rusty half roll alongside, which he eventually found that he needed to complete the task. It was not there – then it was there.

Jott as an isolated paranormal phenomenon

Both Barrington and Jinks found that Jott phenomena never seem to be accompanied by any other paranormal phenomena, such as general poltergeist activity, hauntings or ghosts. Nor is there any association between the number of jott experiences and those who feel that they possess psychic abilities. Jott disappearance or appearance is always noted first by one person and then, according to their personal circumstances, confirmed by others, often by those who have joined in the search.

Jinks is careful to point out that all these shared characteristics do not *prove* that jotts occur, because for 'proof' in the scientific sense you need replicated studies. What they do demonstrate is that after every conceivable normal explanation has been eliminated (and Jinks as a conscientious psychologist examines every possible non jott explanation you can think of), something is occurring that should not occur – but *does* occur. So how does Jinks attempt to explain how jotts can occur?

Jink's hypothesis

For explanation of jotts he turns to the nature of our perceptual relationship to the world around us. Conventional wisdom, says Jinks, sees conscious awareness as merely observing objects in a passive, non-interactive, way as though those objects and the general scene 'out there' are entirely independent of who, or what, is observing them. This is how it feels in everyday life. From behind your eyes you just look out of the window and there it is. Whatever we look at is just there, independent of whether we want it to be there, or not. As he explains it:

> According to the conventional scientific view, consciousness is simply a side effect of physical reality, and the brain no more than a group of cells made up of molecules, which, in turn, are made of atoms that are made from subatomic particles that ultimately consist of a collection of points existing in spacetime, and so on.

Jinks proposes a different interpretation. In quantum physics theory what is known as the 'quantum waveform' exists as an unknowable potential of all quantum possibilities, such as direction of particle spin, or being in two or more places at the same time. This waveform potential becomes actualised in physical reality when the waveform interacts with a measuring device that 'collapses the waveform' into an observable particle or wave according to which the device is designed to detect. Jinks proposes that consciousness can act as a quantum waveform measuring device and 'collapse the waveform' to create the observables of what we see as our external reality. We are not passive observers of the external scene but, at some deep, nonconscious level of consciousness/quantum waveform interaction, we are the creators of what we see through 'collapsing the quantum waveform of ghostly probabilities' that Jinks terms as the "pre-physical substrate' into the physical world of familiar and stable observables.

Jinks speculates that some "deeply fundamental process" of consciousness determines "what the world *should* look like from these pre-physical quantum ingredients" and conscious observers are "merely carrying out the final act of realization". He suggests that the consensual public space in which we live and move is held in a steady perpetuity of existence by the massed conscious observations of those past or present. A car, tree, road, building or landscape, is very unlikely to disappear back into its pre-physical substrate when not observed by anyone because it is sustained by what he terms as a "consensual multisensory landscape" even when not directly observed. But the possibility of this consciousness sustained perceptive reality of an object reverting back into an unseen pre-physical substrate increases when its continued existence is dependent upon only one or two consciousnesses to sustain it.

In such circumstances the consciousness sustained pre-physical-substrate collapse into observed physical continuity is then much weaker than when sustained by massed consciousness. Sometimes the consciousness support that maintains a particular object in observational reality weakens inexplicably and the object disappears from our consensual reality back into its pre-physical substrate, causing Barrington's "spatial discontinuity" and the subsequent jott experience. The jottled object has disappeared from everyone's observation. It hasn't been teleported somewhere else; it is no longer in our mental experience of physical reality. Later, unaware, psychological changes in one or more people may reverse this process and the jott object, now reconstituted from the pre physical substrate, reappears to its owner again just as it was, or maybe as an unrecognised object to someone else. Sometimes it disappears permanently, as Mark's tv remotes seem to have done. But then again. maybe they re-appeared as a 'where on earth did *that* come from?' jott to someone else.

Comment

Unlike other paranormal phenomena discussed in preceding chapters that seem to be caused by psi minded psychokinetic influence, no one appears to have been in a psi state of mind just prior to noticing that an object has disappeared or re-appeared. They were in an everyday state of mind thinking about everyday things when the jott was noticed. In every case their intellectual and emotional response has been one of disbelief and confusion, and they are certainly not in a psi state of mind, post jott disappearance, while searching for it in exasperation, or when wondering where on earth this strange object has come from. The only variable common to the different paranormal phenomena discussed so far is that it has occurred in association with the human mind. This association carries the implication that some property of the human mind is somehow acting as an agent of external effect, and it is this implication that Barrington and Jinks have factored into their respective hypotheses of how jott phenomena can occur.

As the nature of consciousness and its (our) relationship with the physical world remains unknown, we have no idea how our mental reality interacts with physical reality. We know that it must do so somehow, as it directs physical brain activity through the formulation and carrying out of mental objectives, and there seems to be good empirical evidence that in a certain mental state it can exert an external psychokinetic effect. So is there any way in which we can include Barrington's and Jinks' hypotheses concerning the occurrence of jottage with previous speculation concerning other forms of paranormality? Maybe there is.

Three levels of mentalness

I think the term 'mentalness', meaning mental reality as a whole, is a more appropriate term for this discussion than 'consciousness', as 'consciousness', by definition, is a state of mental activity at an awareness of our surroundings. If, for argument sake, we accept that Barrington's and Jink's hypotheses are somehow along the right lines, then the interaction of mentalness with physicalness may occur at three levels, or states, of mentalness.

State 1. The fundamental level of mentalness that interacts with physicalness, maybe at quantum level, to create a mental/physical hybrid of everyday experiential reality. This reality conforms with the three-dimensional physical reality of where objects are, and whether they are moving or not, of classical physics. Sometimes, an individual's mental interaction with physical reality weakens, leading to an object's disappearing from our reality, maybe to return or not.

State 2. Mentalness in the form of everyday consciousness that can exert a psychokinetic controlling effect on the directional activity of the brain, which is dependent upon sensory input for new information about the body and the external environment.

State 3. Mentalness in the form of psi consciousness that can access information directly, as in ESP, and exert an external psychokinetic effect on other living systems and physical objects.

6

Attempts to Conjure up a Ghost to be Called 'Philip' Show the Psychic Strength of the Group Mind

After a group of experimenters spent a year trying to conjure up a ghost, which they intended to call 'Philip', without success, they were ready to admit defeat. Then they tried again, and 'Philip' turned up in a way they didn't expect. What happened questions our present understanding of mind and its relationship to matter.

There are claims in the literature on parapsychology that exerting strong willpower can move very small, light, objects, even when placed inside a glass jar, swing a compass needle away from pointing north, and influence random number generators (RNGs) to generate less random sequences of 0s and 1s during periods of exposure to voluntary willpower. As yet, none of these claims have been considered evidential enough to be incorporated into scientific literature. According to the physical sciences, as well as mainstream psychology and the neurosciences, subjective intention, however emotionally intense, does not, and cannot, exert any direct physical effect on objects. It follows, therefore, that any claim of normally stationary objects moving without the application of some physical force must be in error. In daily life the mental desire to move an object is converted by the brain into instructions to the body to do the physical moving. Mentally willing something to move has no external effect.

The problem for this assumption, backed by daily experience, is that there seems to be experimental evidence demonstrating that when some people, and maybe all people, are in a particular state of mind, objects do move without being touched (see Randall, 1982, for review of research). If, as seems to be the case, this phenomenon, known as psychokinesis (mind moving matter), or PK, is genuine, then something other than consciously applied willpower must be involved.

The 'Philip' case

With this possibility in mind, this chapter is devoted to a re-examination of the 'Philip' case as recounted by Iris Owen and Margaret Sparrow in their 1976 book *Conjuring up Philip: An Adventure in Psychokinesis.* It involved no cheating (confirmed by independent observers and on film), no emotionally disturbed teenagers, no wilful children, no attention seekers, no hidden magnets, no hidden strings, no dim lights, no smoke, and definitely no mirrors.

This experiment, with its completely unexpected outcome, was devised and performed by seven middle-aged, well-educated, sensible, practical people, together with one college sociology student of the same cast of mind (Figure 1). None possessed any skills as a magician or claimed any psychic abilities. But all were determined that if anything unusual did occur it would be noted and recorded objectively.

Figure 1. The 'Philip' Group. Iris Owen (left)
Courtesy of the Survival Research Institute of Canada

Group Members

Iris Owen. Married to Dr A. R. G. (George) Owen. WW2 radio intercept officer, qualified nurse.

Margaret (Sue) Sparrow. Ex WW2 nurse in Canadian Armed Forces. Chair of Mensa for Canada.

Al Peacock. Heating engineer and businessman. Keen photographer.

Lorne. Industrial designer. Amateur astronomer. Member of Royal Astronomical Society (RAS). An expert on old maps, ancient history and oriental philosophies.

Andy, Lorne's wife. Artist (she drew "Philip's" portrait). Also a keen astronomer and member of the RAS.

Bernice M. Qualified accountant. Artist. Keen student of philosophy.

Dorothy O'Donnell. Qualified bookkeeper and accountant.

Sidney, K. College student on sociology course after gap year travelling.

The eight investigators were all members of the Toronto Society of Psychical Research, and their experiment was monitored throughout by independent observers.

Background

The Toronto Society of Psychical Research was a voluntary society affiliated to the New Horizons Research Foundation. Based in Toronto, the Foundation was founded in 1970 by Dr George Owen (1919-2003) to investigate paranormal phenomena. He was a mathematical geneticist and research fellow at Trinity College, Cambridge before he, and his wife Iris (1916-2009), emigrated to Canada in 1970. Dr Owen was also a seasoned psychical researcher, particularly concerning poltergeist activity and psychokinesis (Owen 1964).

The Society was committed to field research into various aspects of parapsychology. Their 'ghost hunting' group investigated reports of hauntings, and soon found that the experience was both unwanted and upsetting to the majority of those concerned. Features common to many of these hauntings were noises such as footsteps, knockings, raps, doors independently opening and closing, untouched objects being moved, and sometimes ghostly figures being seen, causing considerable distress. These effects were usually attributed – by the families or single people involved – to the presence of a ghost of a previous occupant thought to have died in tragic circumstances and unable to 'move on'. When it was a new house or flat it was assumed that a ghost had moved in. In no case did the people involved feel that they were personally responsible for the phenomena; it was happening to them. During one investigation several Society members thought they saw a ghost but, on reflection, remained unsure.

While the group realised that these were real experiences for those concerned, there seemed to be no way of resolving whether ghosts were real in the sense that they existed as entities in their own right, or were hallucinatory experiences, either individual or collective, that were unconsciously generated by the anxieties and beliefs of those concerned. Of the two possibilities, they felt the latter was more likely. To try to resolve this question the Society decided to test the hypothesis that observable ghosts could be created by telepathically shared imagery in the minds of the experiencers.

The question

The experimental question they set themselves was this: could a group materialise an observable thoughtform of a ghost in physical space as a product of their shared imagination? If so, could its materialisation be photographed as objective evidence of its existence?

The scenario

The eight investigators decided that their intended ghost had to be an invented character who, they knew, had never existed in real life, and the story needed to be set in a real-life setting to provide geographical and narrative context as in a historical novel. The period of the English Civil War was agreed upon, and Margaret Sparrow, one of the group members, was delegated to compose the story of Philip Aylesford (1624-1654), a handsome, dashing, well born Cavalier officer who fought in support of Charles I, often acting for the king on many hazardous missions. Here is her original story:

> Philip was an aristocratic Englishman living in the middle 1600s at the time of Oliver Cromwell. He had been a supporter of the king and was a Catholic. He was married to a beautiful but cold and frigid wife, Dorothea, the daughter of a neighbouring nobleman. One day, when out riding the boundaries of his estates, Philip came across a gypsy encampment and saw there a beautiful, dark eyed, raven-haired gypsy girl, Margo, and fell instantly in love with her.
>
> He secretly brought her back to live in the gatehouse near the stables of Diddington Manor, his family home. For some time he kept his love nest secret, but eventually Dorothea, realising that he was keeping someone else there, found Margo, and accused her of witchcraft and stealing her husband. Philip was too scared of losing his reputation and his possessions to protest at the trial of Margo, and she was convicted and burned at the stake. Philip was subsequently stricken with remorse that he had not tried to defend Margo, and used to pace the battlements of Diddington Manor in despair. Finally, one morning, his body was found at the foot of the battlements where he had cast himself in a fit of agony and remorse.

It was decided that the real Packington Hall and Diddington Hall (where Margaret had once lived in the 1960s), both in Warwickshire near Kenilworth Castle, would become Packington Manor as Dorothea's family home, and nearby

Diddington Manor as 'Philip's' family home. Over time the group gathered photographs and local guide books to provide background detail for fictional embellishment. The group was asked to absorb the story and think of Philip' as a real person. So that everyone had the same mental picture of 'Philip'. Andy drew his portrait (Figure 2) and everyone had copies. It was decided that once every century his ghost would be seen on the battlements of Diddington Manor, still desperately searching for Margot to ask her forgiveness, and 1972, when the experiment would begin, would be such a year.

Figure 2. Pen portrait of 'Philip'

The re-examination

For the purpose of this re-examination the events experienced by the group between September 1972 to late 1975, as described by Owen and Sparrow, will be divided into two distinct phases and their implications explored.

Phase One (September 1972 to September 1973)

With the story of their fictional 'Philip' agreed upon, the group commenced weekly, evening meetings in September, 1972, with the intention of creating 'Philip' as a visible ghost, summoned into existence by collective intent. They sat round a table in good light with their hands flat on the table, 'Philip's portrait in the middle, and a growing number of Diddington area photographs on the walls to remind them of the scene.

To attain what they hoped would be the right frame of mind they first meditated together to clear their minds of other affairs, then they discussed 'Philip's' story at length, filling out details of his appearance, dress, personality, family, his relationship with cold Dorothea, his disastrous affair with Margo, the Assizes trial, her being burnt at the stake, his remorse and despairing suicide. They also elaborated on his military service on behalf of King Charles. Each session finished with another meditation, visualising 'Philip' in the hope that he would appear before them in space, rather like a modern hologram.

They engrossed themselves in the history of the Civil War, including music and songs of the period, and the changing fortunes of war between Charles I and Cromwell. By the end of a full year, after some fifty sessions and hundreds of hours together, the group had become very closely bonded and 'Philip' had become like a real historical person. But of 'Philip' himself there was no sign. Despite their united effort to visualise 'Philip' into existence, the experiment had ended in complete failure.

Comment

If the dispirited group had given up after this year of non-achievement they would have fulfilled sceptical expectation that nothing could come of their experiment because, being impossible in principle, it was impossible in practice. However, while debating what to do next, if anything, one of the group had come across the pioneering work of British clinical psychologist Kenneth Batcheldor who, working with two colleagues, provides a full account of his investigations into table turning psychokinesis (Batcheldor,1965-66). For the first few sessions, as Batcheldor and colleagues sat round the table with their hands flat on top, the table tilted and rocked, which was remarkable in itself, but nothing else happened. Then during the eleventh sitting the table rose clear of the floor with all their hands on top. In later sessions this became a common feature, rising up to chest height and often crashing down, even with one table weighing some 60 lbs. The table levitation was confirmed using contact switches attached to the table feet that switched on a light, or buzzed, when the feet of the table left the floor. Later, fellow psychologists Brookes-Smith and Hunt (1970), and Brookes-Smith (1973), repeated Batchelor's experiment and instrumentally confirmed Batcheldor's findings.

They found that group psychokinetic (PK) ability could be achieved by developing what the three investigators described as a 'paranormal skill' that could be acquired by any group. Success in PK was not the result of determined 'make it happen' group willpower, but of a relaxed, shared belief, that table tilting and lifting occurred quite naturally, had happened many times before, and would happen again with them. The experimenters found that when they adopted a relaxed, light hearted, storytelling, atmosphere, together with this shared 'childlike' belief that table turning would occur, then it did occur. The phenomenon fulfilled the scientific criteria of being a predictable experience. This light hearted approach was typical of successful Victorian and Edwardian table turning séances where the gatherings were considered as enjoyable social occasions.

Phase Two (November 1973-late 1975)

The group decided that if this light hearted approach worked with tables, they would continue their quest to materialise 'Philip' as a visible ghost by taking the same light hearted approach. For the first couple of meetings they felt rather awkward and self-conscious when trying to tell jokes and sing songs. But after about three weeks, as they sat round the card table with their hands flat on top, they found a new, light hearted expectancy that 'Philip' would soon materialise as an observable thoughtform, and their cameras were at the ready.

What happened next?

Owen and Sparrow recount what happened next:

> One evening, during the third or fourth session, the group felt a vibration within the table top somewhat like a knock or rap. It is correct to say 'felt' rather than 'heard' because the group were making a degree of noise at that moment, so the unexpected action within the table took them completely by

surprise. These knocks and raps then became louder, being heard by everyone in the group. After checking that no one was doing the rapping as a joke, the group became rather confused as they wanted to see "Philip" as a materialised ghost, and table rapping had never occurred to them." Then the table started to slide about the floor. It moved quite rapidly in random fashion without any apparent purpose. Sometimes the table slid away from under their hands too rapidly for them to keep up with it and they were bumping into each other. This baffling table behaviour of random raps and random movements across a thickly carpeted floor occurred during the next couple of sessions, leaving the group completely nonplussed until someone exclaimed "I wonder if, by chance, Philip is doing this?" Immediately there was a very loud rap from the table top – so "Philip" had come through in a different form from that which we had expected."

Accepting that he had, but still hoping that this was a transitional phenomenon that established his presence before materialising in mid-air looking like his portrait, the group quickly established a code of one knock for 'yes' and two knocks for 'no'. Thereafter they cast their discussion with 'Philip' into a yes/no questioning format in between talking among themselves as usual.

A typical session would commence with greeting each other, including 'Philip', who would respond with a rap. If the group became animated in a discussion that ignored 'Philip' a series of "attention getting raps" would be heard. If they asked 'Philip' questions to which, as their creation, he did not know the answer, there would be several hesitant knocks. If a remark was made that reflected upon Dorothea "the most extraordinary scratching sounds would be heard."

If a particularly good joke was told with much laughter there would often be a "series of loud raps in a kind of rolling effect as if the table was joining in the joke." Besides sliding around the room "the table would tilt in various ways, lifting one, two, or three legs and pivot, sometimes almost dancing" (see Figure 3 with hands on top of the table). 'Philip' was once asked to rap under each of the sitter's hands separately, and each sitter felt a loud rap under the palm of each hand.

Details of 'Philip's' fictional story were steadily filled out over ensuing sessions, with 'Philip' rapping to confirm, or disagree with, proposed new details about his life in accordance with group knowledge and speculation. This is an extract from the tapes concerning the civil war:

> "Did you have your own regiment?" Sid asked.
> (Rap) "Yes."
> "Were you wounded in the fighting?"
> (Rap, rap) "No."
> "I wonder which battles he fought in," Lorne asked.
> "Philip. Did you fight at Naseby?"
> (Rap, rap) "No."
> "Did you fight at Marston Moor?"
> (Rap) "Yes."
> "Would they have had guns of any kind then?" someone asked.
> "They would have had muskets" Lorne said.
> (Immediate confirmatory rap) "Yes."
> "You had musketeers?
> (Rap) "Yes."
> "You fired ball and shot?"
> (Rap) "Yes."
> "Did you prefer firearms?"
> (Rap) "Yes,"
> "Of course he would" someone remarked, "much more effective."

(Confirmatory rap) "Yes."
"I wonder if he ever went spying" Dorothy said.
"Did you, Philip?"
(Rap) "Yes."
"Did you go often?"
(Rap, rap) "No."
"Just sometimes"
(Rap) "Yes."

And so the recorded questions and audible yes/no rap answers went on.

By now 'Philip' as a personality had become integrated into the group as a ninth member who just happened to communicate through raps. Experimentally, they found that 'Philip' would rap whenever, and on whatever, in the room he was asked to rap, including rapping a metal plate hung in the centre of the room and electrically wired to record the acoustic profile of the rap. The raps sounded different according to what was being rapped, and were frequently tape recorded.

To the group the card table now seemed imbued with a life of its own, "rushing across the room to greet latecomers", playfully trapping people in corners and causing general confusion. It would even chase a particular member around the room if asked by the others to do so. During one particularly energetic occasion one of the members exclaimed somewhat crossly, "Well, if you're not tired Philip, I am! Why don't you go right over with your legs in the air, and then we'll have a rest and some cool lemonade." In response the table did just that. The group were standing with their hands lightly on the table and it gently turned and flipped upside down with its legs in the air.

During two sessions in January 1974 a different phenomenon occurred when one leg only was raised up and outwards from the floor by upward distortion of the corner of the table top. It took considerable downward pressure from the group members to flatten the corner and push the leg back down straight onto the floor again. Eventually, the card table became so rickety that the top was coming apart, and after a leg fell off it was abandoned. At one time they had experimented with a heavy refectory type table with solid wooden legs in another thickly carpeted room, but it had careered about so much that they stopped using it for fear of damaging the walls. They now brought this table back into service. A microphone they had strapped under the top of both tables not only recorded the raps, but intense creaking and groaning sounds as if the wooden structure was being placed under considerable intermittent stress and resultant strain ('stress' refers to the forces acting upon a structure, and 'strain' refers to the degree of resulting structural deformation). When they sang jolly songs the table would rap and oscillate in time to the music.

Although 'Philip' was never able to fully levitate the table during these sessions, it seemed to strain upwards as if trying to do so. "Sometimes there would be a curious swirling motion of the table as if he was trying to spin it off. At times the group felt distortions in the table top itself, which took the form of lumps, rather like oranges in size, appearing to rise from the middle of the table as if Philip was trying to raise the table from the middle." Unlike the Batcheldor sessions, this strange phenomenon took place in full evening daylight or with the lights on, and often with independent witnesses present.

In the room known as "Philip's room" there was a frosted glass screen, behind which were coloured bulbs wired to a control panel that the group used to vary the colour and degree of ambient light of the room. While the rest of the house lighting remained steady, 'Philip' would cause one or other of these bulbs to flicker on request. On one occasion, when one of the group was ill and in bed at home, it was playfully suggested to 'Philip' that he should visit him, and at the same time the member heard a series of raps coming from a wall in his room.

During one period when members of the group were feeling unwell with seasonal flu and colds 'Philip's' raps became much weaker than usual, and movements of the table became slow and lethargic. It seemed that, as a creation of their group mind, 'Philip's' mental strength and vitality varied according to the health and number of members present. They found that a minimum of four members was needed to induce the full range of phenomena. In between sessions, whatever table happened to be in use became just an ordinary, inert, table again, but as Margaret Sparrow, creator of 'Philip' said "When Philip was there – even if there was no movement or rapping, the table had a feeling of aliveness, perhaps of vibration, which seemed quite different from its feel under normal circumstances". Members of the groups in Batcheldor *et al.*'s experiments reported similar sensations.

Figure 3. Table turning

The two film sessions

In January, 1974, it was decided that a documentary film to be called *Philip, The Imaginary Ghost* should be made to tell the story of Philip and, hopefully, capture the table raps and movement on film. Because of the risk of physical damage when using the heavy, refectory type table, the group had again abandoned its use, and had decided to use another, lighter, plastic topped table. On this occasion a large room was used with plenty of space for cameras, lights, crew and the group. After the long day's shoot with everything captured on film and everyone packing up, quite unexpectedly "The table levitated fully about half an inch from the floor. It floated a short distance. Although there was a cameraman present it was almost impossible to take a shot of this because of the angle. Everyone agreed that the table had indeed floated" and when asked, 'Philip' rapped in agreement.

In November, 1974, as part of a programme called 'Man Alive', a Canadian Broadcasting Corporation film crew with full arc lights came to film 'Philip' in action. The table rapped in response to questions and moved around as usual, seemingly uninhibited by the bright lights. The group had wanted both films to be made as permanent documentary evidence demonstrating the reality of 'Philip's' psychokinetically caused activity.

The television interview

Following these two films the group were asked if they would take part in a TV discussion programme in the studio in front of a live audience. This would be chaired by the Rev. Lindsay King, a United Church moderator in a local church, together with panellists Dr George Owen and Dr Joel Whitton, a psychologist who had watched the experiment from the beginning, and two other independent observers of the experiment. They were seated on a raised dais, while the Toronto group and table were on the studio floor in front of the dais with the audience behind them.

To quote from their account: "Philip turned out to be what the group had already suspected, a truly ham actor. The table quickly started moving and shot around the studio at some speed. It was soon obvious that Philip felt that his place was up there on the platform with the panellists. The table tried every-which-way to get onto that platform – there were three overhanging steps. The whole procedure was hilarious and the camera crew succeeded in filming the entire proceedings. Philip had to indulge in some quite complicated positioning with the legs of the table to climb onto the platform. Once there it made straight to the moderator who was asked by one of the group to say hello to Philip. He looked somewhat doubtful but did as requested, placing his hand on the table and saying "Hello, Philip". He was obviously surprised, as were the television crew and audience, when a very loud rap came from under his hand. He continued to ask questions and received raps in reply. These were all recorded and filmed. The programme, televised by Toronto City TV, was broadcast as "The World of the Unexplained". In December, 1974, four members of the group accepted an invitation from Cleveland, Ohio, to demonstrate the table raising effects to an audience of psychologists and physicists. They reported that "the phenomena were very good. On two occasions one of the physicists sat on the table and was thrown off – quite violently."

A similar experiment, initiated by a different group within the Society, was also carried out during 1974. They invented a story of a French-Canadian girl named Lilith who went to France during WWII and became a member of the French Resistance. After many adventures, including a tragic love affair, she was caught by the Gestapo and executed as a spy. This group, meeting weekly, followed the same procedure as the Philip group, drawing a picture of their heroine and developing a complete history. Within five weeks they obtained conversational rapping responses from the table and table movements. Phase Two of the "Philip" experiment had now been replicated by another group with similar results.

Taken together, these two group experiments provided, in one case, filmed and documented evidence of psychokinetic activation for which, at present, there is no explanation. They could not have happened according to physics – but they did. At the end of 1974 the Toronto group decided to end the experiment. They felt that as two films and a television video now provided a permanent record, they wanted to be free to become involved in other research. The table now stayed as an ordinary table, and 'Philip' never returned.

A review

A table cannot move or emit raps on its own because it is a rigid, inert, physical structure that has no internal volition. It would be the equivalent of lifting itself up by its own proverbial boot laces. The question, therefore, with regard to Phase Two is this: was it all done by deliberate, or non-aware, pushing, turning, and lifting the table? Was the rapping done by one, or more, of the group? If so, then problem solved, as there was no psychokinesis, just deliberate cheating, or non-aware rapping and table pushing and carrying. But during filming the hands of group members are on top of the table (Figure 3), and if they are not grasping under the edges of the table they cannot lift or turn it. In fact, as a further precaution against unintended pushing, they often placed doilies under their hands as the doilies would slip if they tried to physically move the table. Again, because they often had to try to keep up with apparently random movements of the table, including tilting and gyration, they often lost contact. If they were physically doing it, such considerable physical effort would be very obvious to observers and on recorded film, including members becoming out of breath. Owen and Sparrow make the point that no one felt mentally drained of energy by the end of a session as if it had somehow been sucked out of them, and this raises a fundamental question: if the group were not, somehow, mentally supplying the considerable physical energy involved in the erratic movements of a table around a room, what was the source of the energy? What, or who, was doing the rapping in response to questions? We need to consider in more detail what occurred under the heading of *Non-normal table behaviour*.

The three main classes of psychokinetic table phenomena can be considered separately.

1. Acoustic raps

The rapping was in response to verbal communication and could be predicted as occurring as one rap, two raps, or a scratching sound, according to whether the question is being answered by a 'yes' or a 'no', or a 'don't know'. Raps were in response to a greeting, or used to express agreement or dissent during group discussion. Raps also occurred as apparent attention seeking. 'Philip' was also able to elicit a rap from elsewhere if asked to do so, as in the metal plate that was hanging overhead, and the wall raps heard by one of the members when ill in bed at home. This implies that acoustic energy was momentarily transferred by 'Philip' into those separate structures. It seems as if the raps were a form of communication with whoever was talking to 'Philip' and whoever, or whatever, the 'Philip' was that 'inhabited' the table when in session. This is what would be expected if 'Philip' was a projected creation of the group mind because he shared their common knowledge.

1a. Acoustic rap characteristics

Scientifically speaking this is crucially important. If the acoustic profiles of the raps differ in frequency amplitude and duration from those caused by knuckle or pencil taps then no one is cheating. Acoustic analysis showed that the vibratory period from the start to finish of control taps using knuckles or a hard object showed a sharp rise and quick fall, whereas the "Philip" raps increased in volume and then fell. With a control tap or knock there would be an almost instant rise to peak vibratory amplitude coincident with the instant moment of applied, percussive, energy, whereas the amplitude of a 'Philip' rap peaked more slowly as if increasing in vibratory amplitude from within before dying away. The two rap sources also sounded very different, as in blind hearing tests the sharp sound of the control tap could easily be distinguished from the more rounded sound of a 'Philip' rap. This also fits in with the comment that a vibration was sensed under a hand before the rap was felt and heard. These acoustic differences between PK raps compared with applied taps have been noted by other experimenters and are discussed further in chapter seven.

2. Table activity

This often seemed like unpredictable childish behaviour. Sometimes, as if trying to accomplish a predetermined goal as in climbing the steps onto the dais in the TV programme, or rushing across the room to greet someone, 'Philip' exhibited an apparent degree of self-activation, often escaping control of the group. While language response by rapping obeys social convention, humans have no experience of trying to move around as a four-legged table. If the table had all its weight on its legs when it tried to move, then thick carpet friction against the feet of the front legs would cause it to topple forwards. But this did not happen. In fact, when the group tried to manually reproduce sliding table movements, they couldn't do so because of the high frictional resistance of the thick carpet. This was especially true with the heavy, refectory type table with its thick legs.

When the group put objects on the table and then physically tipped it, the objects would slide off as expected. But when a request was made to 'Philip' that they should remain where they were placed during table tipping and movement they did not slide off. They seemed held to the surface by an attractive force.

3. Localised table structure distortions

Owen and Sparrow said that "At times the group felt distortions in the table top itself, which took the form of lumps, rather like oranges in size, appearing to rise from the middle of the table as if Philip was trying to raise the table from the middle." These distortions then spontaneously disappeared.

4. Targeted bulb flicker

If all the houselights remain steady after being switched on, then the voltage (electrical pressure) throughout the mains circuit must be a constant across all the light bulb filaments connected to it. Any changes of light output from individual bulbs can occur only if there are localised changes in voltage pressure, or changes in the resistance of the local connecting wire, or across the bulb filament itself. With all things being electrically equal this just cannot happen but, apparently, it did when they requested 'Philip' to do it.

All of these non-normal table phenomena occurred only when, in Margaret Sparrow's words "Philip was there" and the table had "a feeling of aliveness, perhaps of vibration, which seemed quite different from its feel under normal circumstances."

The group state of mind

The one mental variable that has remained consistent throughout the first four chapters is that the seemingly impossible, non-normal, phenomena, occurred only when those involved had transitioned from the everyday state of mind into the psi state of mind. This is not an explanation, but it tells us in what state of mind we should be when searching for an explanation. In this case, during Phase One, the group remained in their everyday state of mind, consciously willing Philip to appear as a materialised ghost, and feeling increasingly discouraged and frustrated when, despite their united mental effort, he failed to do so. Conversely, during Phase Two, they were in a relaxed, happy, childlike 'whatever will happen will happen' psi state of mind when 'Philip' first attracted their attention by an unexpected rap.

The Psi Mind

From the evidence of the relationship between being in the psi mindset, and the occurrence of external, non-normal phenomena, it seems reasonable to infer that the psi state of mind possesses mental properties not present in the everyday state of mind. The latter seems solely dependent on what the bodily senses can detect as incoming information, and what the body can be physically instructed to do. It cannot directly act upon, or receive information from, the external world except through the intermediary of the senses. Conversely, there seems to be good empirical evidence that the psi mind can do the following:

1. Receive information directly in the form of extrasensory experience (see my companion book *Telepathy, Clairvoyance and Precognition* for case studies).
2. Interact directly with the physiology of other living systems as demonstrated in the non-placebo studies presented in Chapter One, and healer/healee EEG concordance during a successful healing session described in Chapter Two.
3. Induce a calming effect in the minds of other people as presented in Chapter Three.
4. Directly 'inhabit' or imbue and subsequently control otherwise inanimate, freely movable structures in which, as in this case, they can respond to questions by yes/no raps. On this point it is worth requoting Margaret Sparrow, creator of "Philip" who said: "When Philip was there – even if there was no movement or rapping – the table had a feeling of aliveness, perhaps of vibration, which seemed quite different from its feel under normal circumstances".

5. While apparently imbued with the psi mind an object, in this case a table, can, on request, act on material structures elsewhere to produce raps, and affect local electrical current flow as in causing lightbulbs to flicker while other lights remain steady. An object can act free of the constraints of gravity acting on its mass.

When those involved revert from their psi state of mind back to their everyday state of mind the non-normal physical phenomena cease. When, for example, the Toronto group members agreed to finish a session and move on to other things, the table reverted to being an inanimate structure fully subject to physical laws. The same applied to the tables in Batcheldor *et al.*'s experiments.

A psychokinetic event

In his 1982 book *Psychokinesis: A study of paranormal forces through the* ages John Randall provides a review of many carefully designed experiments, including strain gauges and contact switches, where non-normal psychokinetic phenomena occurred beyond reasonable doubt. He defined a psychokinetic event as follows: A psychokinetic event is the occurrence of any external physical phenomena which cannot satisfactorily be explained in terms of known physical forces, and seems to involve the participation of some kind of mental entity or entities.

I think this definition can now be reworded to be more specific with regard to the mental circumstances: A psychokinetic event is the occurrence of any external physical phenomenon which cannot satisfactorily be explained in terms of known physical forces. It occurs only in the presence of a person, or group of persons, when they are in a psi state of mind.

Discussion

In everyday life, and in science, everything is defined by the nature of its interaction with everything else: in effect, what it can do, what it can interact with, and, just as importantly, what it cannot do or interact with. Magnets, for example, can attract certain metals but have no effect on other metals, and cannot exert any effect on anything non-metallic such as wood or plastic. If pivoted, as in a compass needle, the compass always swings to point north, and a magnet moving across a wire can induce an electric current.

The wide range of physical and biological sciences methodically investigate the what, where, when, how and why of our physical world, and can now provide an explanation for most phenomena from the birth of the universe some 13.7 billion years ago, to the birth of the earth some 4.5 million years ago, to the evolution of life from some 3 billion years ago to the present day. Based upon the evidence of no direct mental interaction with anything external when in the everyday state of mind, which is taken as the mental norm, the sciences are agreed that mental processes cannot directly affect anything else. This seems to be confirmed by the fact that our thoughts and emotions, however intense, are not directly detectable by any physical instrument.

What EEG electrodes and modern brain scanning devices detect and record are patterns of physical brain activity that *correlate* with different forms of mental activity, but are not the thoughts and emotions themselves. Our thoughts and feelings are known only to ourselves as first-person experiences because being non-physical, so non-detectable, they are not available for study as self-existing, independent, phenomena.

As we cannot objectively detect and measure the mental nature of mind, including consciousness, we do not know what mentality is, so we cannot define it despite the fact that we experience ourselves as mental beings. We cannot, therefore, say in advance what mentality is capable of doing, or not doing. We can only go by objective evidence of what happens in the material world when we know that a particular form of mentality is involved. This indicates, for example, that when the everyday state of mind is dominant, its psychokinetic effect is limited to acting upon the brain to act through the body to achieve mental objectives. The fact that we still have no idea how, does not alter the fact that it does.

When in another state of mind, termed here the 'psi state' to distinguish it from the everyday state, it not only retains its primary, psychokinetic interaction with the brain but, as these opening five chapters have shown, it can somehow act across space to exert objective psychokinetic effects. These range from affecting the metabolic activity of other living systems, to subliminally calming other people's minds, and effecting the movement of, and affecting the structure of, non-living, normally inert, movable objects such as tables. If telepathic communication is accepted as a fact, then the first two external affects seem to be reasonably understandable as acting upon responsive living systems, but the third psychokinetic affect seems to be much more difficult to understand because there is nothing responsive in the inanimate nature of a wooden table.

Nevertheless, as evidence of external psychokinetic effect is the subject of this investigation, preconceptions of what is possible or impossible need to be set aside, and the implications of what was experienced and recorded as happening need to be explored.

Observed external psychokinetic effects

Movement

The tables often tipped to balance on two legs and occasionally on one leg in the absence of any applied physical force. Sometimes a table would turn upside down without an applied physical force. On occasion this tipping force was so strong that it dislodged someone sitting on the table. The table moved freely around the room, changing in speed and direction of movement in the absence of any applied physical force.

Localised change of structure

The molecular structure of the wooden, or plastic, table top, became locally malleable in the form of raised bumps and then returned to localised rigidity. The same occurred when, with three feet on the floor so the table top was level, one table leg swung diagonally outwards as the attached corner of the card table top bent upwards. This distortion was so strong that it required heavy manual pressure to push it back down.

Vibration

Instances of localised internal vibration increased to a level of acoustic amplitude that could be heard as raps. These raps differed in acoustic profile from applied knocks.

All of these psychokinetic phenomena transgressed the following laws of physics.

The Psi Mind In Action

Mass, gravity, and Newton's Laws

Like all material objects having mass, tables are subject to gravitational attraction between their mass and the mass of the earth (which we experience as weight), and to Newton's Three Laws of Motion. These are:

> First Law of Motion (Inertia). An object at rest remains at rest unless acted upon by an external force.
> Second Law of Motion (Force). The rate of acceleration of an object depends on the mass of the object and the amount of force applied.
> Third Law of Motion (Action & Reaction). For every action, there is an equal and opposite reaction (recoil).

What was observed and experienced during psychokinetic table movement can be summarised as follows:

1. The effect of gravity was nullified to a degree equivalent to the weight of the table. There was no frictional drag on the thick carpet during horizontal movement. The tables glided about freely as if on wet ice. When a table rose vertically, gravity was overcome as if not operating.
2. For the first law and second law of motion, the necessary external force seemed to be replaced by an internal directional force that controlled horizontal momentum (mass multiplied by velocity). This momentum was experienced by group members when a table pushed against them and they pushed it away, and caused concern in case the travelling momentum of the heavy table caused it to damage the walls.

3. The third law of action and reaction seemed to be nullified during acceleration from rest, and deceleration to rest. The tables did not push *against* anything from which to accelerate from rest, or *against* anything to slow down and reduce momentum, so there was no equivalent external reaction to their action.
4. Balance. The tables were able to maintain their balance when tilted and poised on two legs, or on one leg, even during movement. This means that they retained their centre of gravity within the remaining area of gravitational stability which, when tilted, was no wider than the narrow edge, or corner, of the supporting two legs (Figure 3), or one leg. This is equivalent to an upright pencil remaining vertically balanced on its point both when still, and during change of speed and direction.
5. The normally inert, rigid, structure of the transverse grain of the table framework and flat table top attached to it became locally malleable, as when one of its legs swung outwards and lifted up. This curved distortion was also associated with a localised upward force that resisted downward pressure.
6. Localised raised tabletop mounds occurred that flattened out again.
7. Localised rapping sounds were heard when an apparently internally generated vibration reached sufficient acoustic intensity to be heard in the audible range of around 800-1000 Hz. These were heard as rapping sounds, not percussive tapping sounds, and were responsive to audible questions.

Questions

If the above is accepted as describing what occurred, and that these occurrences occurred only when the group were in a particular state of mind, then there is something that we are not yet understanding about the nature of mentality. Who, or what, was the invisible 'Philip' that was seemingly created and recreated into existence only when members of the group were in this mindset, but apparently non-existent when they were not? The group members felt no depletion of energy in the sense of undue mental fatigue, even when the heavy table was careering around, so what was the renewable and sustainable source of energy that counteracted gravity and Newton's Three Laws? Margaret Sparrow said that "When Philip was there – even if there was no movement or rapping, the table had a feeling of aliveness, perhaps of vibration, which seemed quite different from its feel under normal circumstances" Maybe, in a search for answer, the clue lies in the table's having a feeling of "aliveness".

A very tentative hypothesis

In *Seven Lessons in Physics* (2016) and *Reality Is Not What It Seems: The Journey to Quantum Gravity* (2017) the theoretical physicist, Carlo Rovelli, explains through a brilliant use of analogy, metaphor, and diagram, what we now know about the universe, ranging from the bewildering world of the infinitely small of quantum physics to the infinitely large of space and time. Our everyday, cause and effect reality, operates for objects somewhere between these two extremes in terms of size, but all is dependent on the quantum world for its existence. He does this so well that even non-numerate readers like the present writer can feel that they understand something of the awesome wonder of the universe in which we live. He explains how, from 1900 onwards, theoretical physicists Planck, Boltzman, Einstein, Heisenberg, Schrödinger, Dirac, Hawking, Feynman, Gell-Mann and many others contributed to our present understanding of the universe, especially the quantum world of subatomic particles and fields – filled with its elementary particles of protons, neutrons, electrons, quarks, muons, Higgs particles etc. that, when composed as stable atoms, creates our observable universe. The fundamental equations that have been found to govern the universe are summed up in what is known as the Standard Model of particle physics. They are so accurate that predictions based on these equations are correct to the nth degree. Everything in the world of physics, from particles to fields, has a basic unit that defines it in its relationship to everything else. In the Standard Model it seems that there is nothing left over. All is accounted for, and that is the problem.

Mental agency

On page 3 of *Seven Brief Lessons in Physics* Rovelli says, "There are absolute masterpieces which move us intensely: *Mozart's Requiem*, Homer's *Odyssey*, the Sistine Chapel, *King Lear*." But there is no equation in the Standard Model for mental intensity. So, if mental intensity exists, something is missing from the Standard Model. It is not complete.

It is proposed that what is missing from the Standard Model is the existence of mental agency, for which there is no physical definition. Agency is defined as possessing the ability to act autonomously and freely. Something that possesses mental agency has the ability to define objectives, know how to achieve those objectives and know that they have been achieved. Such concepts do not apply to the physical universe. Nothing in the physical universe possesses any degree of self-autonomy beyond the equation(s) that has been found to govern what it can, and cannot, do. We define the difference between being "inanimate" and "animate" by the absence, or presence, of mentalness. The former is subject to physical processes devoid of agency, while the latter possesses some level of mental agency.

Rovelli points out that we cannot, in principle, know the nature of something in isolation from how it interacts with other things. It is the manner of interaction that defines it. In the same way, one way of defining the nature of mentality is by its interaction with the physical world, and this is determined by its agency of affect. In the case of all animals with a brain, mentality's primary agency of psychokinetic affect is directing the activity of the brain in its role as controller of all bodily functions including the musculoskeletal system. It is through directing the brain's control of the latter that mental agency, in deciding mental objectives for bodily survival and the goals necessary to fulfil them, achieves its objectives. It does this in the everyday state of mental agency, but, as this and the preceding chapters have shown, this is not the only state.

When, in Phase One, the Philip group decided to try to create a mid-air materialisation of 'Philip', they created a mental agency of group affect. What they did not realise was that in using their everyday state of mind of consciously directed will power to create him, they were using a mental agency limited to mind-brain psychokinesis only.

When, in Phase Two, they entered the psi state of mind, even though they did not realise it, they had now engaged a mental agency of external affect that could affect matter. They still wanted to create a spectral image of 'Philip' substantial enough to be light reflecting, but their lack of success may indicate that air was not the right medium (this inference, of course, leaves the status of ghosts and apparitions unresolved).

It seems that what was required, as Batcheldor and many other experimenters had discovered, was a physical structure substantial enough, and in this case mobile enough, to be "imbued" with their mental agency. As with other experimenters, this happened to be the wooden table they were sitting round with their hands flat on top. Acting as a focal point it somehow, initially unknown to them, became 'informed' by their externalised mentality of affect. The how remains a mystery, but the empirical evidence clearly indicates that it did.

Thinking speculatively, to enable the table to achieve free movement and generate rapping responses, their group psi seems to have interacted with the molecular structure of the table, maybe in the form of a mental field, psychokinetically interacting with its physical nature. If this tentative hypothesis is on the right lines, this must have happened at subatomic, quantum level. It is proposed that their psi energy suspended, or neutralised, the forces in quantum nature that create the property of atomic mass and, in consequence, the mass of the table.

By suspending or neutralising the table's mass, their psi also neutralised its gravitational attraction to earth (its weight) and its momentum during movement. The table had become weightless, allowing it to float free as Newton's Laws of motion no longer operated. This hypothesis seems to be supported by the fact that none of the group complained of being drained of energy during horizontal movements of the table as no energy had been expended in physical effort to move it. The 60lb (27kg) table used in some of Batcheldor's experiments did not weigh 60 lb as it rose in the air with their hands on top of it, but did when it crashed down.

During periods of group psi it seems that the table became a psychophysical entity, retaining its physical shape and integrity, but obeying psychokinetic intention instead of responding to external physical forces. At the moment when this transform occurred, Margaret Sparrow said that the table had "a feeling of aliveness, perhaps of vibration, which seemed quite different from its feel under normal circumstances." From Owen and Sparrow's descriptions of its activity, and as captured on film, when acting as 'Philip' the table would seem to have become a secondary centre of psychokinetic intention. It sometimes acted free of the group, and sometimes even acted in opposition to the group, as when a leg was elevated outwards as its corner bent upwards and they had difficulty in pressing it down. In another example, when four members of the group went to Cleveland and a member of the audience sat on the table, 'Philip' repeatedly threw him off as if 'he' could intentionally exert a physical force when 'he' wanted to.

When in psychokinetic communication with the group, 'Philip' could generate raps in answer to questions, and apparently could generate raps in other structures elsewhere. An alternative explanation for the latter may be that it was the group who, unknowingly, psychokinetically generated those raps by imagining what they expected would happen when asking 'Philip' to do it. The same might have been the case when asking 'Philip' to flicker the lights. None of it makes sense according to the Standard Model of particle physics, but it seems that the Standard Model only applies in the absence of mental agency: in this case the psychokinetic agency of the psi mind.

Current neuroscience theory

Monism

The current theory in the neurosciences and mainstream psychology, is that brain activity and mental activity are two sides of the same material coin. In effect, the two act as one, operating within the confined substance of the brain. This theory, known as neural monism, denies the theory of dualism. The latter states that mental activity including consciousness and all our emotions, is different in kind, not degree, from the bioelectrical energy of the brain. If neural monism is correct in that everything takes place within the brain, and if the evidence for external psychokinetic effect is accepted, it is difficult to understand how the brains of the 'Philip' group managed to neuro-kinetically activate the tables, including responsive rapping.

Dualism

If, instead, the concept of the physical brain's being in correlated, psycho-neural control by the mental agency of our minds is accepted as fitting the psycho-neural facts better, then the empirical evidence for external psychokinetic effect seems more understandable in principle. When we are in the everyday state of mind our mental agency is in psychokinetic control of the brain, but when we are in the psi state of mind our mental agency can operate to external psychokinetic effect. In either case, and it really is important to remember this, we don't have the slightest idea of *how* this occurs, but the empirical evidence in both cases clearly demonstrates that it does.

Note: It is important that you judge for yourself whether the table phenomena occurred as described. Here are the links to the only two videos on which some of the original film has been transcribed. The longer extract includes a very lucid presentation by Iris Owen of what occurred.[5]

7

Acoustic Analysis Confirms the Temporary Existence of 'Eric' the Andover Wall Rapper

The case discussed in this chapter has been chosen to show that strange events can, and do, occur in ordinary family homes. 'Eric', as the family called whatever it was that 'lived' in a bedroom wall for eight weeks, answered questions by rapping, had some 'temper fits' with loud thumping and banging, then disappeared. The family involved with 'Eric' were Mr and Mrs Andrews (pseudonyms), and their six children Maria (20), Kevin (19), Gary (17), Steven (15) Theresa (12), and Mark (10), who had lived in their four bedroom house in Andover, Hampshire, UK, for five years. Built in the 1960s on an abandoned gypsy caravan site, it was one in a terraced row of council houses. The terrace was punctuated at first floor level with through alleyways to the back gardens, and the bedroom that Maria and Theresa shared was situated over an alleyway.

For purposes of discussion 'Eric's' relationship with the family, as investigated and recorded by Dr Barrie Colvin (2008), will be divided into the friendly and cooperative period, and the short, aggressive periods.

Friendly and cooperative period

Good Friday, 12 April, 1974, had been a normal day for the family. Maria and Theresa went to bed in the late evening and chatted about this and that. They had single beds placed on either side of their bedroom, with Theresa's bed next to the dividing wall. While they were quietly chatting they became aware of light tapping sounds coming from the dividing wall. At first, they took no notice, as they assumed it was their neighbours doing some DIY, but they slowly became aware that the taps seemed to relate to their questions and answers. Puzzled, because they were talking far too quietly to be heard by anyone next door, they asked whatever was doing the tapping to reply to questions with one tap for 'yes, two for 'no', and three taps if it did not know the answer. To their astonishment, it duly did all three. It did so again the next evening, and continued over the following evenings with their siblings joining in the fun of questions and wall tapping replies. While their parents, particularly Mrs Andrews, sometimes joined in, they remained rather hesitant as they could not account for the wall tapping phenomenon.

News soon spread around the local community, and on the 26th April an item was published in the *Andover Advertiser* under the heading 'Mystery ghosts making their lives a misery', rather overstating the case and adding the plural for effect. The story came to the attention of Dr Barrie Colvin, Council member of the Society for Psychical Research. He had a particular interest in investigating reports of apparent poltergeist activity, and as it was an ongoing case he decided to contact the family. With a PhD in X-ray crystallography of polymers, and as founder and managing director of IFS Chemicals Ltd, he was normally immersed in the hard-headed world of scientific research, and took the same scientific approach when investigating apparent poltergeist phenomena.

Colvin met the Andrews family on the 28th April, sixteen days after the tapping first started. He explained his interest and told them about other cases of poltergeist phenomena. After some initial reluctance they said that they would welcome his help, and were willing for him to undertake an investigation into what was happening and the circumstances in which it occurred. The Andrews seemed to be a happy family with no history of psi phenomena and no previous knowledge or interest in the subject. Maria was an outgoing personality with a steady boyfriend, while Theresa was quieter and more reserved. Colvin says that to him 'there was a feeling of loneliness about her and, although she was attractive, her friends were few.'

Widening the answering format

Because the yes/no/don't know tap code rather limited what could be asked of whatever was doing the responsive tapping, it was suggested that answers could be given by spelling out each letter of an answer by the number of taps equal to the numerical position of the letter in the alphabet. For example, as 'e' is the fifth letter there would be five raps with an emphasis on the last rap, and the wall tapped back in agreement.

Using this rather slow system, the source of the tap said that its name was Eric Waters, that he had died many years ago and his bones were under the floorboards. Extensive inquiries by local historians, including records of two families of Waters, failed to find anyone with that name who had even lived in the area. Eric was most responsive when Theresa was lying still on top of her bed in full view of everyone. The sessions would begin by asking Eric if he was there and receiving an answering tap. Those present would be sitting on Maria's bed or standing facing Theresa and the wall. One very early session went as follows:

> "Are you living or are you dead?"
> "Why are you here?"
> "When did you die?"
> "Where are you?"
> "Which football team is going to win the F.A. Cup final?'

Eric answered, saying that he was dead, but as to when he died, and where he was now, he didn't seem to know and became confused. He did, however, correctly predict that Liverpool would win the F.A. Cup, and in another session that Leeds United would win the F.A. League, but apparently these would have been easy guesses anyway. Mr Andrews hoped that he could forecast horse race winners but in this Eric was not very successful.

By now, neighbours would sometimes call in to witness these sessions, as did the local clergy and a medium from the local Spiritualist church, who rather unnerved the family by saying that she sensed Eric's bones were under the floorboards. Even the police called in, with everyone eager to solve the mystery but to no avail. To Mrs Andrew's surprise, Eric was most responsive when she asked the questions on behalf of everyone else and Theresa was lying on the bed. If Mrs Andrews counted the taps, and got the alphabetical letter wrong, Eric would immediately tap twice for "no" and start again. Interestingly, they noticed that Eric often anticipated her wrong answer as if he knew what she was about to say. Later on, when doing tests, if Colvin held up a numbered card that everybody could see, but wall-based Eric could not see, or asked Eric how many people were in the bedroom, Eric would tap the right answer, often in a rather hesitant, adding up sort of way.

To eliminate the neighbours as the source of the wall taps, Dr Colvin asked Eric if he could tap his answers from different areas of the dividing wall, which he did. Eric was then asked to rap on the wooden bed head or metal bed frame, which he also did. The taps sounded characteristic of whatever was being tapped. Colvin also noticed that Eric's tap sounded different from when Colvin tapped on the same surface with his knuckles or a pencil. Eric's taps were more a softer sounding rap than a sharp tap. He also noticed that when he placed his hand lightly on the wall or bedhead he sensed a slight vibration under his hand that preceded the sound of the rap as if it was somehow being generated within the wall or bedhead itself. This vibratory sensation preceding the sound of a rap had been noted by investigators in other cases. Besides recording question and answer sessions with Eric's responsive raps, Colvin also did microphone recordings of Eric's raps and his own knuckle or pencil taps for later acoustic comparison.

During this period Colvin invited Dr Reinhart Schiffauer, Senior Scientist of Egham Research Laboratories, Surrey, to attend a couple of sessions to photograph the spot where the raps were coming from to see if a film might reveal something their eyes were missing. Although they used high speed black and white film as well as colour and infrared, and Eric was cooperative throughout by responding with definite raps, nothing unusual was captured on film.

On one occasion after talking with Eric, Colvin and Schiffauer had inadvertently left the recorder running while they went down to talk to Mr Andrews, leaving Theresa and her mother in the bedroom. Mrs Andrews asked Eric if he had any further message for them, and heard a single firm rap indicating that he had. She asked for the first letter and Eric rapped nine times indicating "I", he then continued to rap out "I am here to rest and stop my bones from rotting". Later, when listening to the recording, they heard that when Mrs Andrews miscounted and said the wrong letter, Eric immediately rapped twice for no. For example, on one occasion Eric did 20 raps with an emphasis on the final rap. When Mrs Andrews asked "S?" Eric did a two rap "No" at the same moment that she corrected herself by saying "T" and Eric immediately rapped once.

After the three short hostile periods to be described below, friendly relationships were resumed until Dr Colvin's final visit on Monday, 10th June. He had received a call from Mr Andrews saying that Eric's responses had been getting fainter over the previous two weeks. At 7.30pm that evening they all entered the bedroom and Mrs Andrews asked:

> "Eric, are you there?"
> *(No answer)*
> "Eric, have you got a message for us?"
> *(No answer)*

After some 15 minutes of trying to contact Eric, but with no answer, Theresa said that she sensed he had gone forever, and would never return.

The five aggressive periods

During the 15 days up to the 28th April, when Dr Colvin first visited, Eric had been friendly and cooperative. But at 8.15pm on the Monday, 29th April, Mr Andrews telephoned Colvin to say that they had been kept awake all night by

Acoustic Analysis

Eric. The knocking sounds had become very much louder and despite numerous requests Eric would not stop. The family felt for the first time that Eric was purposely trying to frighten them. They, in turn, were starting to resent Eric. When Colvin visited them on Tuesday, 30th April, he found that the family mood had changed, with Mr Andrews feeling tired and irritable. The previous day had been as normal until about 6.30pm when, with Theresa and family downstairs, there was a sudden, heavy, loud, bang, followed by a series of loud raps. Kevin and Gary raced upstairs to find the rapping coming from the wall. When Kevin asked, "Is that you, Eric?" there was a loud thud which shocked everyone. Then there came another series of loud sporadic knocks. This was the first time that Eric had acted spontaneously, in this case by causing a loud wall bang in the absence of Theresa, who was downstairs with the others, so the bedroom was empty.

As Eric usually started to communicate only after Theresa had gone to bed, Colvin returned about 8.30pm and stayed downstairs while Mrs Andrews joined Theresa and asked Eric if he wanted to talk to them. He had obviously calmed down and replied with a gentle rap. She then asked Eric "Is it all right for Barrie to come into the room?" He replied with a loud knock and Colvin quietly entered to join the others. He observed that Theresa was lying on top of her bed and Maria was in her bed with a light cover over her. A question-and-answer session then followed. When Mrs Andrews asked Eric how old he would be if he was still alive, he replied with a long series of slow raps that became more hurried then petered out. It had been noted before that Eric seemed to have little understanding of time. It was during this first visit that Colvin placed his hand on the wall and felt the vibrations preceding the rap. When Eric rapped on the headboard and metal frame of Theresa's bed as requested, Colvin again felt the vibrations before the rap. As Theresa said she was feeling tired the session ended with Mrs Andrews saying "Goodnight Eric" and receiving a responding soft rap.

For the next four days Eric was friendly as usual and then, in the evening of Saturday, 4th May, Mr Andrews phoned to say that Eric was getting very aggressive again, with very loud raps as if he was feeling angry. Again, Eric was acting without Theresa's presence in the bedroom. This time the raps turned into loud knocks merging into bangs so loud that people could hear them down the street. Colvin visited them the following morning. They told him that during the previous evening, Eric said that he wanted his bones dug up and reburied in a graveyard. When Kevin took over the questioning Eric refused to respond and remained silent for the next half hour. Kevin, feeling increasingly exasperated, then asked:

"Are you there, Eric?"
(No answer)
"I think you've gone away".
(No Answer)
"I don't think you ever existed".
(Single loud bang)
"Eric, I don't believe you were ever a real person".
(Another loud bang)
"I think you are a liar, Eric".

This was followed by a series of increasingly loud knocks that would stop and start again. There was no way of stopping them, and they rapidly became so loud as heavy bangs that they could be heard outside again. Eventually they ceased, but the family, now very much on edge, had little sleep that night, and felt they had had enough. Next morning, with Colvin present, Theresa asked Eric if he was there but received no response. An angry Kevin then shouted, "Eric, I think you are a bloody great liar!" The immediate response was a very loud knock. Colvin saw that Theresa was now looking very shocked, pale and tearful. Kevin, however, continued shouting "You are a liar Eric, and you are not under the house". This was followed by a series of very loud knocks and Mrs Andrews, now distressed, left the bedroom. While Kevin continued to provoke Eric, Colvin realised that the knocks were not coming from the wall this time but from the headboard of Theresa's bed. Placing his hand on the headboard he could, again, clearly feel the vibrations building up in the wood before they heard the loud rap.

The next day, Monday, had passed reasonably peacefully, but, when Colvin rejoined the family on the morning of Tuesday, 7th May, Kevin had again decided to provoke Eric, and Eric had obviously decided to retaliate, as the banging sounds emanating from the wall were quite deafening. Some 20 people had gathered in the alleyway under the bedroom to listen, and the banging was so loud that Colvin could hear it in the garden from some 50 yards away. He asked those present to put their hands on the alleyway wall, and everyone could feel the vibration preceding every bang. Eric continued to bang for about 30 minutes until, to the relief of everyone present, the banging ceased. Thereafter there was no more hostility, and peace was restored until the 10th June, 1974, when Eric, after sounding weaker and weaker, responded no more.

Comparative acoustic analysis

Scientifically speaking, what would place the Eric phenomenon beyond all possible doubt would be an amplitude waveform analysis of Eric's raps and Colvin's applied taps, demonstrating that the two were consistently different. In May, 1985, Dr Colvin submitted his tapes to Bruel and Kjaer (B&K), specialists in acoustics, to be digitised for acoustic analysis by their applications engineer, John Shelton, using Adobe Audition software. Also submitted were good quality acoustic recordings made during other poltergeist investigations where raps were a feature. For poltergeist aficionados, these were from *Souchie/Sauchie* (1960), *Thun* (1967), *Schleswig* (1968), *Pursruck* (1971), *Ipirango* (1973), *La Machine* (1973), *Enfield* (1977), and *Santa Rosa* (1988).

With regard to the Andover inquiry, Figure 1 shows the shape of the amplitude waveform created by a percussive knuckle knock on the wall next to Theresa's bed. As would be expected, the moment of suddenly applied, percussive, energy is converted to an initial, maximum vibratory waveform that is then damped by the physical properties of the wall into dying vibrations.

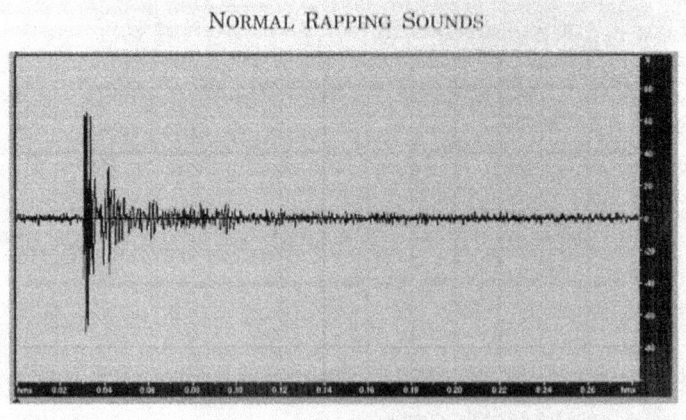

Figure 1. Waveform of knuckle on wall.

Figure1. Percussive knock on the bedroom wall (reproduced by permission)

ACOUSTIC ANALYSIS

Figure 2 shows the shape of the amplitude wave form created by an answering Eric rap. In marked contrast to the knuckle knock, the amplitude of the Eric vibration increases from zero and remains more sustained before slowly fading away. The two sets of waveforms are visually distinct from each other. On comparative listening, tests, a knock sounds like a sharply percussive 'tap', whereas Eric's rap sounds more like a soft 'r' that builds up before dying away.

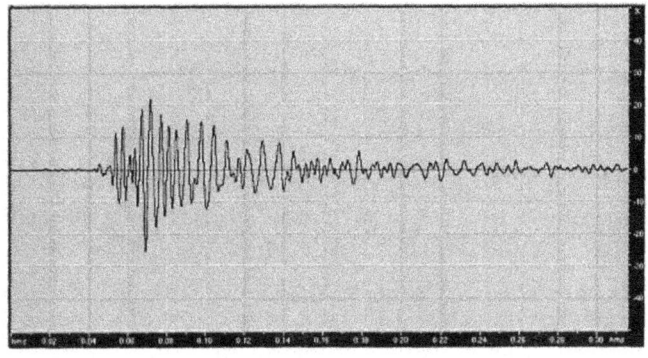

Figure 7. Andover (1974).

Figure 2. Eric's answering wall rap
(reproduced by permission).

Each of the recorded raps from the other investigations showed the same rising amplitude waveform as if the acoustic energy was coming from within whatever was the source of the rap. To doublecheck these findings and eliminate any possible error, further experiments were performed, using a range of hard to soft percussion instruments hitting a range of different surfaces. All failed to duplicate the slow rise of Eric's waveform, as all recorded an initial, maximum amplitude, waveform.

A summary

At this point it might be useful to summarise what occurred during the 8-week Andover case, including the results of the acoustic analysis.

1. For a period of 8 weeks, from the 12th April until about the 10th June, 1974, the Andrews family experienced an unexpected occurrence of raps, knocks, and sometimes loud to deafening bangs, emanating from the adjoining wall next to Theresa's bed or her bedhead. They were not caused by anyone tapping or hitting either the wall or bedhead.
2. They appeared to have been initiated in answer to quietly spoken conversational questions between Theresa and Maria. At first, they were in the form of one rap for "Yes", two raps for "No", and three raps for "Don't know". Later, these responses were supplemented by answering using numerical counting of the letters of the alphabet until a word had been spelt out, with the end number receiving an emphasised rap.
3. The source of the rapping said that its name was Eric Waters, and his bones were buried under the floorboards, but official and social records failed to find anyone with that name living in the area. That Eric's bones could have been under the floorboards seems very unlikely, as they would have been discovered when digging the foundations for the house.
4. When in a cooperative mood Eric would change the source of his rap from the wall to the wooden headrest and metal frame of Theresa's bed on request. He responded best when Mrs Andrews

Acoustic Analysis

asked the questions and Theresa was lying flat on top of her bed, but would answer other people.

5. There was often a degree of wilfulness exhibited by Eric as to when, and how loud, he would make a rap, and whom he would respond to. Sometimes he would not respond at all.
6. On five separate occasions Eric appeared to be angry, creating thunderous bangs that could be heard in the alleyway and down the street. On these occasions Theresa was in the house but not in her bedroom.
7. Dr Colvin and family could feel the wall or headboard vibrate before hearing the rap, and Eric's raps sounded softly different from sharp knuckle or pencil taps.
8. Acoustic waveform analysis demonstrated that the waveform profile of the Andover rapping differed from that caused by a sudden percussive force. The latter caused an instant rise to maximum waveform amplitude, while the raps exhibited a slower rise to maximum amplitude. This finding was in line with the acoustic analysis of close miked recordings made during other poltergeist investigations.
9. The Andover rapping began for no apparent reason, and ended for no apparent reason by dying away over a final fortnight into permanent silence.

Eric's acoustic phenomena

While, as Dr Colvin pointed out, Eric's acoustic phenomenon is described in terms of 'taps' 'raps', 'knocks' and 'bangs' as this is how they sounded, this is not what Eric was actually doing. He did not apply any external, percussive energy, as if he was situated next to the wall or bedhead and hitting it. Dr Colvin did not feel any sudden impact pass through his fingers into the wall or bedhead. He felt a rising level of vibratory energy entering his fingers from the surface that he was touching, which terminated in a sound closest to that of a rap. It was as if a localised area of the molecular structure of the wall, or bedhead, generated an increase in vibrational energy before its release as an acoustic sound. Only earthquakes show an almost identical waveform, as the strain in a continental plate caused by huge tectonic stress is released as the rock is suddenly deformed.

It is as if Eric was a temporary, psychokinetic extension of Theresa's personality of which she was consciously unaware. If so, this implies that Eric was an externalised form of mental energy that could generate localised levels of vibratory molecular stress that was released as acoustic energy from quiet 'raps' to thunderous 'bangs' radiating from the whole wall. The question remains: what was the source of Eric's energy?

Discussion

Who, or what, was 'Eric' remains unknown, but that the phenomenon of Eric occurred is beyond all reasonable doubt. Firstly, there is the testimony of the Andrew's family, together with the testimonies of Dr Colvin and Dr Schiffauer as external investigators. Secondly, there were tape recordings of question-and-answer sessions in which Eric's responding taps could be heard. Thirdly, there are close microphone recordings of headboard- and wall-emitted Eric raps, together with percussive knuckle and pencil taps available for comparative acoustical analysis, and fourthly, there is the B&K Adobe Audition waveform analysis demonstrating that Eric's raps differed from percussive taps. Such raps cannot spontaneously be emitted from an untapped wall or bedhead. It requires the application of applied physical energy. That they did occur beyond all reasonable doubt implies that something other than the laws of physics must have been involved.

That 'something other' appears to have something to do with Theresa. It was as if Eric was a psychokinetic extension of Theresa's personality of which she was consciously unaware. Although, this seems to be so, it leaves the source of Eric's energy, from answering raps, to thunderous bangs, unexplained. Theresa could not possibly have generated such energy for Eric to use, as she would have been completely drained by the banging and would have collapsed. But this did not happen.

In his discussion Dr Colvin points out that as everything and everyone in the bedroom could be observed in good light, deception would have been very difficult to conceal. As he saw it, only two sources of the Eric phenomena seemed possible. Either incarnate, as in a living person, or discarnate, as in some form of unknown entity. Colvin felt that the circumstances and relationship of Eric with the family ruled out the latter, as no answering rapping occurred unless Theresa was in the house, and occurred most frequently when she was lying flat on her bed. Also, as Eric never indicated that he knew anything outside general family knowledge as known and understood by Theresa, it seemed that Theresa was the source.

Although this seems to be the most likely option, it does not suggest how it occurred. Unlike other cases where a highly emotionally distressed teenager, usually a pre to adolescent girl, seemed to be the source, or focus, of poltergeist activity (see Gauld and Cornell, 1979 for a major study). Theresa seemed to be a quietly normal, twelve-year-old girl not given to emotional outbursts. Her air of apparent loneliness as it appeared to Dr Colvin, implies a rather introspective turn of mind compared with her older, more apparently extrovert, siblings, but no more than that.

Theresa

This part of the discussion can only be speculative because we do not know anything about her thoughts and emotions at the time concerning what was going on in her life. We don't know anything about her relationships with fellow pupils or teachers at school, or other children who lived along her street, or what books she was reading and thinking about. We don't know about her relationships with her four brothers or her parents at the time, beyond an apparently close one with Maria. We also do not know anything about the dynamics of family relationships, whether between the parents, or between one or both parents and children, or between the siblings themselves. Most family dynamics have their quiet periods and emotionally disturbed periods, especially with teenagers in the family, and we do not know what had occurred during that Good Friday. This means that we don't know what Maria and Theresa were discussing on that Good Friday evening; perhaps she was feeling in an unusual state of mind.

To her own surprise Mrs Andrews seemed to be more able to interact with Eric than anyone else in the family as long as Theresa was present. Theresa appeared to act as an apparently passive intermediary between the rest of the family and Eric when lying on the bed, as, apart from the initial question and answer session that Good Friday evening, she never seemed to ask Eric any of the questions.

On the occasions when Kevin became exasperated with Eric, shouting at him and saying that he didn't believe he existed, Eric responded with uncontrollable loud bangs that reverberated into the alleyway and street. The family became very agitated, possibly with much shouted argument, and Theresa, caught in the middle, became very upset. She may have felt very protective of Eric and angry with Kevin for provoking him. As for Eric, if he somehow 'fed' on her emotions as a secondary personality, he may have been responding to her distress in the only way he could by furious wall banging. Eventually, it seems that whatever in Theresa's nature had become the unwitting source of Eric, assuming this was so, it diminished and disappeared. Eric faded into non-existence, and ordinary, everyday, family life resumed.

The psi mind

In my previous book *Telepathy, Clairvoyance and Precognition*, I proposed that non-normal, or non-everyday phenomena, such as telepathy, clairvoyance, and precognition occur only when those involved are in a psi state of mind rather than an everyday state of mind. I have made the same proposal in the preceding chapters of this book with regard to the occurrence of non-normal phenomena such as the non-placebo effects and reduction of crime during periods of group TM-Sidhi. In brief, my theory is that our everyday state of mind, which is essential for practical survival, is limited to its interaction with our brain and its control of our body. This is the site of primary psychokinesis. By this I mean that our everyday mindset affects the physical activity of our brain, but only our brain. The outside world is not involved.

But there is another state of mind that I have termed the psi state. This retains its primary psychokinetic interaction with the brain, but also includes the ability to exert a direct, external, psychokinetic effect on material objects in the outside world. I have proposed that the evidence for this is that non-normal events occur only, it seems, when those present are in the psi mindset. I suggest that this seems to have been the case with Theresa and Eric during those 8 weeks in 1974. We do not know if Theresa, now in her 60s, has had other ESP or PK experiences in her life.

In their review of some 500 well recorded cases of poltergeist phenomena, psychologist Alan Gauld and parapsychologist Tony Cornell (Gauld & Cornell, 1979) found that in about two thirds of these cases an emotionally disturbed teenager, usually female, appears to have been the focus. Given that there must be millions of similarly disturbed young women, as well as young men, over the generations there should be millions of recorded instances of poltergeist phenomena occurring in family homes, prisons, hostels and bedsits, and even more in times of war. Instead, there seem to be only hundreds, at most, in the literature. But even if thousands go unrecorded, the obvious question is, why the disparity in numbers between stressed out teenagers where nothing unusual happens, and those stressed-out teenagers where what is termed as poltergeist activity occurs.

Maybe the reason why, in the majority of cases, the emotional stress is released in angry physical activity is that it remains within the emotional boundaries of the everyday mindset. In the relatively fewer cases where poltergeist phenomena occur, their emotional distress enters their psi state of mind and finds release as an externalised psychokinetic effect. Maybe this is what happened to Theresa, but, as we will never know what she was inwardly experiencing over that 8-week period, we will never know for certain. [6]

8

A STOLEN HARP FOUND BY MAP DOWSING LEADS TO DR ELIZABETH MAYER'S REVELATORY INVESTIGATION INTO PSI PHENOMENA

This chapter is based upon Dr Elizabeth Mayer's personal experiences of psi phenomena, her follow-up interviews into psi experiences, her assessment of her research findings, her overview of psi phenomena and a proposed theory to account for it.

The intriguing dowsing story of Dr Mayer's stolen harp and its return, her encounters with four psychic intuitives, and her own very strange psi experience, was discussed in my book *Telepathy. Clairvoyance and Precognition*. These are recapped here, but what was not discussed were the results of her subsequent inquiry into psi phenomena, and proposed theory of psi developed in collaboration with Professor Robert Jahn and Dr Brenda Dunne, that culminated in her 2007 book *Extraordinary Knowing:*

Science, Skepticism and the Inexplicable Powers of the Human Mind, with a foreword by leading physicist Freeman Dyson. Her book was the outcome of some thirteen years of methodical investigation, and was completed just before her untimely death in January, 2005, at age 60.

Dr Mayer was an Associate Professor of Psychology at the University of California, Berkeley. She taught at UC Medical Centre, San Francisco, and was a Fellow on the Board of the International Consciousness Research Laboratories, Princeton University. As a psychoanalyst, researcher and experienced clinician she had authored over 50 papers, sat on many committees and editorial boards, attended international conferences and was a respected training and supervising analyst for the American Psychoanalytic Association. When, in 1992, the harp recovery episode occurred that "irrevocably changed my familiar world of science and rational thinking, changed the way I perceive the world and try to make sense out of it", she was in her late forties, married with two children, lived in Oakland, San Francisco, and was in the middle of a successful professional career. We will follow the sequence of astonishing events that changed her mind as they unfolded in 1991/92.

The stolen, traced, and recovered harp

In December 1991, her eleven-year-old daughter Meg was in a theatre in Oakland playing her harp in a Christmas concert. Meg was already a skilled harpist, using not the standard, large, pedal harp but a small, easily carried, and very valuable harp. At some time during the concert in Oakland, a large port in the Bay Area, she must have left the harp behind the scenes unattended, because when she went to collect it and put it back into its case the harp had been stolen. Two months of police inquiry over Christmas and New Year, and even a local CBS TV news story led nowhere. By late February 1992, Dr Mayer and family had become resigned to the likelihood that this was just one more unsolved theft among many others in the Oakland Bay area. At home, a heartbroken Meg had rejected all other suggested harps and remained inconsolable.

While discussing her feelings of helpless frustration with a close friend, Dr Mayer was rather taken aback to hear her friend suggest that, as all else had failed, she had nothing to lose by contacting a dowser to see if he, or she, could locate the harp. Knowing nothing about dowsers beyond a vague picture of them walking around holding forked sticks looking for underground water, she agreed out of politeness, but with no personal conviction because it was obviously impossible. As she had no idea how to find a reputable dowser she asked her friend to make enquiries on her behalf. She, in turn, contacted the American Society of Dowsers (ASD) and was given the telephone number of Major Harold McCoy, President of ASD, who lived in Fayetteville, Arkansas, some 1800 miles (2100km) east of San Francisco.

With no expectation of success, as none of this made any sense at all, but driven by maternal desperation, Dr Mayer phoned Major McCoy, then aged 61, and said that she had heard that he could locate lost objects by dowsing, told him how the harp had been stolen, and asked if he could locate it. Major McCoy replied, "Give me a second and I'll tell you if it is still in Oakland." A few moments later he said "Well, it is still there. Send me a street map of Oakland and I'll locate it for you."

At this point we must pause and review the situation. At the time Oakland Bay had a population of some 400,000 people, many of whom were, as they have always been, itinerant passers through. At the time, the city was considered to have a high rate of theft and, of course, contained hundreds of streets. Major Mc Coy, some 1,800 miles (2100km) east in a town in central America, has received a phone call out of the blue from someone he does not know, about a stolen harp he did not even know existed until then. Yet, with only a moment's dowsing reflection, he states that without doubt it is still in the Oakland area, and if she would send him a street map he will, not might, but will, locate it for her, a seemingly impossible task. Dr Mayer says that while she felt "somewhat encouraged by his friendly, cheerful, heavy Arkansas accent" she remained unconvinced. He could not possibly fulfil his promise, as it was just not possible.

The map was sent overnight, and two days later Major McCoy phoned Dr Mayer to say that he had located the harp, stating that, "It's in the second house on the right on D----------Street, just off L— Avenue." We can imagine that he has spread the map out in front of him and methodically 'asked' the dowsing implement, often a short pendulum, but Major McCoy used a pair of hand-held rods, whether the harp is in area A or B. He interpreted their swing across each other, or just pointing ahead parallel to each other, to mean either 'Yes' or 'No'. Moving methodically across the map squares, he narrowed down the 'Nos' until they crossed in a 'Yes' square, then he checked street by street until they crossed over this particular intersection and this exact location. However, this still amounted to no more than a bold statement of location. Dr Mayer was still faced with the problem of finding out whether he was correct. Knocking on the door and politely asking whoever answered whether they had stolen a small harp and could she have it back, was unlikely to meet with 'Yes I did, please come in'.

The area of Oakland that McCoy had identified was unknown to Dr Mayer but, feeling she must now follow this lead through, she drove there, noted the street and house number, and went to the police to tell them that she had received a tip that the stolen harp was there. They were completely uninterested, saying that such a vague tip did not justify a search warrant. They also said that they were closing the case, as the harp was a very portable and marketable item, and the thief would have sold it on long ago.

Still having to face her devastated daughter, Dr Mayer felt that there must be some way of finding out if the harp was at that address, so she decided to flypost the immediate block of houses, thereby not being specific to that address, offering a reward for its safe return.

Three days after flyposting a man phoned her to say that he had read the flyer, and gave her an accurate description of the harp. He said that his next-door neighbour had shown it to him, telling him that he had recently 'obtained' it. He offered to get it returned to her and, after a fortnight of telephone negotiations on the proposed deal, it was arranged that she would meet a teenage boy at 10:00pm in the car park of a nearby all-night Safeway close to that address. They met; he asked, "The harp?" Dr Mayer nodded, the exchange took place, and she headed joyfully home with the undamaged harp safely tucked in the back of her station wagon. Some 25 minutes later, as she turned into her driveway, she thought *This changes everything* (her italics).

Discussion

It is beyond all reasonable doubt that the loss and recovery of the harp happened as described as it was family and public knowledge. Assuming prior scepticism of all things allegedly psi, be it telepathy, clairvoyance or precognition, when you think about it, would this experience have *changed everything* for you? Would it have convinced you that psi, demonstrated in this case by an example of incredibly accurate remote viewing using a map, could no longer be dismissed as impossible in principle, so impossible in practice? If not, then you must have spotted the sensible, non psi explanation that successfully evaded Dr Mayer. Did she really miss something here that lets the psi sceptic off the psi hook?

The only possible non psi explanation would seem to be that Major McCoy knew someone in the criminal fraternity of Oakland who knew the thief, knew where he lived, knew that he still had the harp, and knew that Dr Mayer would contact him. To pursue this line of inquiry we need to know something about Major McCoy, and assess whether it was likely that he had friends in the criminal underworld of Oakland and was party to some elaborate piece of deception.

Alabama born Harold McCoy (1932-2010) was an ex-army man. He had completed 24 years military service as an intelligence officer, before retiring with the rank of United States Army Major in the late 1970s to live in Fayetteville, home to the University of Arkansas. Over the years he discovered that he had a gift for healing, together with a talent for finding lost objects through the medium of dowsing. In the mid 1990s he obtained a grant from the State of Arkansas to found and direct the Ozark Research Institute (ORI), Fayetteville, Arkansas, as an educational, scientific, charitable non-profit organisation, chartered by the State of Arkansas to conduct classes and research into 'The Power of Focussed Thought'. To this day all funding remains channelled to the same end. On a personal basis he always refused any payment, however successful the outcome of an inquiry, as he believed that his gift came from God and should be offered free of cost.

In one of his articles on the ORI website he explained what happened when a caller asked for his help when trying to find a lost object. As he entered the mindset of dowsing

A Stolen Harp Found by Map

and commenced to dowse, it would appear in front of him as a clear mental image while he tracked down its location, and he could then give the caller directions for finding it even when, as in Dr Mayer's case, the caller and object were over a thousand miles away. In terms of conventional science and psychology this is a truly ludicrous statement to make. Later, when Dr Mayer asked Major McCoy how dowsing works, he told her there was no rational explanation, saying, "The rods just show what your subconscious mind knows already". According to him they aided dowsers to enter into this subconscious, intuitive, knowledge that they already possessed by providing the focus that brought the knowledge into consciousness. He went on to say that some master dowsers find that they no longer need a dowsing implement as they have learned the ability enter into that state of mind and 'know' directly. Given the circumstances, it does seem rather unlikely that Harold McCoy knew whom to contact in the Oakland criminal fraternity.

If one accepts his account, then one is faced with accepting that McCoy did exactly what he said he did as described by Dr Mayer. Somehow, he 'knew' exactly where, in a teeming city with hundreds of streets and thousands of houses and flats, the harp was hidden. We are left, therefore, with four indisputable facts:

1. That Meg's small harp was stolen from a theatre in Oakland during a Christmas concert.
2. That, some 2 months later, McCoy pinpointed the exact house where it was hidden.
3. That he achieved this feat from some 1800 miles (2100 km) away.
4. That acting upon this information Dr Mayer was able to negotiate the safe return of the undamaged harp from that address.

In this form of psi known as 'direct knowing' it seems that distance is an irrelevant factor. The only conclusion would seem to be that some people, including the late Harold McCoy, actually possess this faculty of 'direct knowing' in the form of 'remote viewing' or, to use its older term, 'clairvoyance'. For him, the state of mind in which 'direct knowing' occurs, was induced through the technique of dowsing. As this mental feat of detection is not possible through the use of any of the accepted five senses, some people must possess some other sense, operating on different principles, through which such mentally direct information can be obtained. This sense is called psi.

Known traditionally as the 'sixth sense', the faculty of psi appears to employ different forms of 'direct knowing' as appropriate. Evidence to support this hypothesis that some people, if not all people, possess a functioning psi faculty comes from thousands of well documented personal experiences, together with extensive laboratory data, including many successful studies on remote viewing (see Radin, 2006, Carter, 2007, and Vernon, 2021 for literature reviews, and Wilkins and Sherman, 2004, for an account of sustained telepathic rapport over five months).

That we do not, as yet, have an explanation as to the nature of psi and how it works is not a valid reason to reject the hypothesis if the evidence demands that such a faculty must exist. After all, we have no explanation as to the nature of consciousness and its qualia properties of thought, memory, emotion and sense of self that are at complete odds with the quantitative properties of the physical universe including the brain. Yet we accept that the self-aware mentality of consciousness exists on the anecdotal basis of daily personal experience.

Given the unchallenged facts of this case it would seem reasonable to accept that the faculty of psi exists, and the extensive data claimed to be evidence of psi in operation should be taken into account when exploring the nature and properties of mind. If so, then it follows that psychology texts need to include psi as a legitimate area of psychological inquiry. It is not a psychological outlier as the term "para" psychology" implies, but part of psychology like memory or vision, that comes under the heading of 'psi'.

An acute cognitive dissonance

Initially, Dr Mayer was certain that if only she could analyse what had happened just a little more clearly, step by step, she would find the sensible, everyday, answer to how Major McCoy knew where the harp was hidden. She also discussed it with her colleagues. But, despite sleepless nights, no such answer revealed itself. In not doing so she said that "It changed my relatively established, relatively contented, relatively secure sense of how the world adds up. If Harold McCoy did what he appeared to have done, I had to face the fact that my notions of space, time, reality, and the nature of the human mind was stunningly inadequate." She realised that the intellectually comfortable world of conventional scientific and psychological thought had no answer. Even worse, it said that as such a feat was not possible in principle, it could not have happened in practice.

The problem for Dr Mayer was that it *had* happened in practice beyond all possible doubt, so seeking an explanation within a scientific paradigm that said, in effect, that it had not happened because it could not happen, left Mayer in a state of what psychologists term 'acute cognitive dissonance' between a personal "I know it happened" and an intellectual belief system that said "No it didn't; you must be missing something." So how to resolve this cognitive dissonance? Where to turn for answers?

The psi literature

As conventional psychology could not help, the only alternative was to explore the literature on a subject that she had previously dismissed without inquiry as flaky, pseudoscientific nonsense, that no sensible person educated in any of the sciences, including psychology, could possibly believe. This scientifically disreputable subject was Parapsychology, so Dr Mayer found herself studying something called Extrasensory Perception (ESP), and something called Psychokinesis (mind directly affecting matter), or PK, as manifestations of a hypothetical faculty called Psi, so known collectively as psi phenomenon. She read articles and books by bold researchers who, despite their conventional scientific training, had taken the professional risk of inquiring into psi and were known as parapsychologists, mainly concerned with laboratory studies and statistical analysis of findings. They worked alongside psychical researchers who investigated anecdotal accounts of apparent psi experiences, undertook field studies of ghosts, apparitions, and poltergeists, and carried out surveys of people's beliefs in paranormal phenomena. To Dr Mayer's astonishment she soon discovered that the literature on parapsychology contained "a significant bank of well-conducted, scientifically impeccable research."

As the story of the harp spread amongst her medical and psychoanalytical colleagues, they, again to her surprise, started to unburden themselves of telepathic, clairvoyant, and precognitive experiences that they had tried to dismiss as chance coincidence yet knew, with an inner discomfort they resolutely ignored, that, somehow, they were not. For the first time they felt they could safely share their uncomfortable dissonance between their unwanted experiences and intellectual denial of them. As Mayer put it "by email, snail mail, at conferences, in seminars, hall corridors, or at dinners" their stories poured out. "My patient walked in and I knew her mother had died – no clues – I just knew, instantly." "I woke up in the middle of the night like I heard a shot; the next day I found out that it was exactly when my patient took a gun and tried to kill herself." "I suddenly felt my partner's son was in trouble. I called my partner and it worried him enough that he tracked down his son. He had been in a bad car accident and my partner got there just in time to make a decision about surgery that probably saved his life." A child psychologist, whose brother had died by drowning many years earlier, was treating a 4-year-old girl on a day that happened to be the anniversary of his death, and she was thinking of him and re-imagining what had happened. In the middle of her play the girl suddenly looked up at her and said, "Your brother is drowning; you have to save him," and then went back to playing with her toys. As the psychologist said afterwards, "the hairs stood up on the back of my neck," None of these puzzling experiences made any rational sense to those who experienced them, yet invoking chance coincidence as the 'sensible' explanation did not offer any real explanation. These experiences carried an inner certainty that just did not feel like chance.

By 1997 Mayer had so much material that she and a close colleague, Carol Gilligan, professor of social psychology, New York University, inaugurated a discussion group called 'Intuition, Unconscious Communication and Thought Transference' that met during the biannual meetings of the American Psychoanalytic Association. Anyone who wanted to join had first to submit a written account of an apparent psi experience, which they were unable to explain in conventional terms.

They were flooded with carefully written, and, where possible, verified accounts including, as word spread, from medical practitioners and highly skilled nurses whose sudden, unaccountable awareness of their patient's condition and prognosis for good or ill, exceeded anything prognostic in their medical work-up. The floodgates had truly opened. Their accounts, her notes on them, and her follow up research into the circumstance when such experiences seemed most likely to occur, filled more and more file drawers.

In 2001 she published a posthumous paper by Robert J Stoller MD, a prominent psychoanalyst, relating dreams recounted by his patients that reflected what was happening in his own life. After completing it he had decided not to publish, as he realised that he risked his professional status through derision at his gullibility by his peers. In one such dream a patient of his "saw an older man crash through a glass partition as he was carrying a heavy object during a party." During that same weekend Stoller crashed through a glass partition while helping to transfer some chairs. In another dream a patient "saw a new invention based upon a large concrete pole on which prefabricated rooms could be hung." That same weekend Stoller was talking to an architect who told him of a brand new idea of a large concrete pole on which prefabricated rooms could be hung. Another patient reported a dream in which he walks through a home where a new sunken bath had been installed, and there was an initial in the soft cement. Stoller had just had a sunken bath installed and had found, to his intense annoyance, that someone had inscribed an initial into the new cement. This article resulted in another flood of responses detailing similar experiences of patient and psychoanalyst interactions that could not be accounted for by knowledge that either one possessed about the other prior to the event.

Intuitive knowing beyond chance explanation

As part of her inquiry Dr Mayer consulted many self-proclaimed psychics, or intuitives, without success, finding that their practised generalities conveyed no evidence of anything more than clever guesswork and cold reading of a client's social background, behaviour, and responses to leading questions. Then, yet again, as with the harp, "everything changed" when she consulted four particular psychics, or intuitives, recommended by friends and colleagues who had received accurate readings. These were Deb Mangelus, Ellen Tadd, John Huddleston, and Helen Palmer. She held many accurate, tape-recorded sessions with each of them, and the following is a summary of her experiences and what they told her about themselves when in the intuitive, or psi, state of mind.

Deb Mangulus

A friend recommended Deb Mangulus, as an intuitive who had made an accurate diagnosis of his medical condition over the phone despite knowing only his first name. She lived on the east coast at Cape Cod, some 2700 miles from Oakland on the west coast, so their environment and their social worlds were poles apart. Now in a very sceptical frame of mind indeed, Dr Mayer arranged a telephone session, giving only her first name and saying that she had heard of her through a friend. At the time of this session Dr Mayer and a colleague were interviewing applicants for a managing directorship in an arts organisation. They were vacillating whom to choose between two women who were complete opposites in appearance and personality, as well as in their relative strengths and weaknesses.

When the session started Mangulus told her that the reading would be audiotaped and the tape posted to her.

She then gave Dr Mayer a choice between telling her what was troubling her, which some clients wished to do, or staying silent while she 'tuned in' and talked as thoughts and images came to her. As this would be the crucial test Mayer chose the latter. Deb Mangulus said "Fine. I'll take a few seconds *to be sure that it is you I am seeing* and then I will say whatever comes to me" (my italics). She then told Dr Mayer that she was trying to choose between two very different women for a managerial post and was finding it very difficult. She went on to say that she saw one as fiery and playful, had trouble with words, and was probably not always reliable, whereas the other was responsible, dutiful, and very orderly. She then said of the latter "I keep seeing her hands and they are clasped in her lap. I simply *can't* get her to unclasp her hands." Her description of the two women and their personalities had been very accurate, the fiery one was visually fiery with a huge head of red hair, but it was her "seeing" the other woman's hands remaining clasped in her lap that really stunned Dr Mayer. Throughout the two hour interview this applicant had sat still with her hands clasped tightly in her lap. Mayer had been so struck by this unmoving posture that she had made a note of it for discussion with her fellow interviewer.

Ellen Tadd

When Mayer went for a reading with Ellen Tadd she, as usual, used her first name and nothing more. Ellen sat next to her while holding and looking at her right hand: a procedure, she said, that activated her clairvoyant reading of the client. During her reading she was very accurate concerning a difficult relationship that Mayer was having with one of her daughters, including the reasons why it was happening, and how to resolve it. At another reading Mayer decided to give Ellen a specific test. She had the references she needed to choose between some colleagues to join her for a research project, so she gave Ellen a list of the top five names and asked her to describe their strengths and weaknesses. Readings for the first three names and the fifth name on the list fitted well with what Dr Mayer already knew of each candidate, but Ellen was unable to make any connection with the fourth name, a man whom Mayer had never met but had been chosen on the strength of his published research in the same area. Ellen tried more than once to contact him but gave up, saying that she "simply couldn't find him." Some four weeks later, having received no reply to her invitation, Mayer phoned his number, only to be told that he had died very unexpectedly some six weeks previously, two weeks before she had met Ellen Tadd for the test reading.

Dr John Huddleston

John Huddleston was a member of an academic discussion group that included Mayer. This group met monthly to exchange ideas. Beyond meeting him socially on these occasions there was no other contact as they worked in different branches of psychology. Hearing from colleagues that besides his academic career, he also had a good reputation as a professional intuitive, she became curious and arranged a telephone session with him. Much of what he said concerning family and current issues she found accurate, until he described a close family member in terms that was very disturbing and, in her opinion, completely unlikely. She told Huddleston that his reading concerning this person must be wrong as she knew him far too well. It was absolutely impossible that he was the sort of person who would do what Huddleston said he was doing, but

Huddleston politely refused to budge, saying that he just knew he was right. Some twelve days later, to the stunned shock of herself and the rest of her family except the member involved, she discovered that everything Huddleston had said was accurate. She does not say what it was.

Helen Palmer

On hearing a taped reading with Palmer concerning a client whom Mayer knew well, including the family and family dynamics, she was so impressed by its accuracy that she arranged a telephone session, giving only her first name. During the reading Helen said that Mayer was trying to write a particular paper, but was becoming increasingly frustrated with it as it just would not fall into place. This was true and she could not understand why she was finding it so difficult. Palmer then went on to describe what she 'knew' was the article that Mayer subconsciously wanted to write, and, as she was listening to Palmer, she had a mental image of the paper. This was written with ease over the next two months, was duly published (Mayer, 1996), and was completely in line with Helen Palmer's description.

Entering into the intuitive, or psi, mindset

In response to Mayer's follow-up inquiries into their state of mind just before, and then during, a reading, their answers implied that they each experienced a similar transition from the everyday state of mind to the intuitive, or psi state of mind.

During Mayer's first telephone call to Deb Mangelus she had, in effect, described the moment of transition when she said, "Fine. I'll take a few seconds to be sure that it is you I am seeing and then I will say whatever comes to me." Later, she told Mayer "I know what I know about the other person because I go where they are. I really am seeing with their eyes when I read them."

Dr Huddleston told Dr Mayer that for him the intuitive mindset was one of

> putting my everyday self aside and *entering into* a *relaxed focus which has a calm clarity, and a receptive quality. I'm in communion with the client and they are very easy to see, but I don't merge with them in order to read them. Doing a reading is as effortless as opening a gate and stepping into a new landscape – the client's health, relationships, family, joys, challenges and future – they are all there* (my italics).

Helen Palmer (who has written extensively on the intuitive mindset) said that for her, Intuition operates from a very different state of mind from ordinary consciousness: quite decisively different. 'You lose awareness of the room, your body, your face. That all goes but there is a separate awareness that stays. You read another person accurately because you are them; you know them from the inside because you've stopped being separate'.

She said that she had learned to leave her everyday state of mind in which we remain separate from other people, and, once in her intuitive state of mind, she entered into a state of clairvoyance in which "I can locate people at a distance or at different points in time within a greater reality that embraces us both."

Concerning her intuitive state of mind, Ellen Tadd said that on taking her client's right hand to do a reading, she left the everyday world in which we are all separate from each other and entered into "a clairvoyant state of oneness with the client during which you get a very profound knowing."

The Psi Mind In Action

Dr Mayer's involuntary experience of psi knowing

After discussing what her four intuitives had told her concerning their state of mind in which they do their reading Mayer goes on to say: "Suddenly, and bizarrely, I remember a strange, disassociated moment: a moment when, for the first and only time in my life, I might have experienced exactly what that knowing is like." Sometime previously, Mayer's husband had given her 17-year-old sister a present of a gold watch after she had come to stay with them. To her husband's exasperated annoyance her sister repeatedly mislaid the watch and they found themselves searching for it yet again. On this occasion, when Mayer had returned from work before her husband, she found herself and her sister becoming increasingly frantic to find it before he came home. They methodically checked every room, stairs and passageway that she had been in during the day without success. There was nowhere else to look; and then something very unexpected happened "that was unlike anything I had ever experienced. I was standing in our upstairs hall near the closed door of my husband's study.

> I walked into his study: deliberately, intentionally, but with no awareness of volition on my part. It was as though I was watching myself in a slow-motion film. I walked straight to a closet in the far corner of the room, a closet I'd entered maybe twice – if that – over the course of our entire marriage. As I walked I wasn't aware of thinking, of deciding, or of choosing to do, any of the things I was doing or was about to do. I was just doing them. I bent down – again it felt absolutely deliberate – and reached deep into the closet behind a row of shoes, then behind some boxes behind the shoes. My hand went directly to a small leather case in the very back

A Stolen Harp Found by Map

corner. I lifted the case, stood up, and opened it. Inside was the watch. Weirdly, I felt neither surprise nor excitement. I simply expected it. I then walked out of my husband's study, called for my sister, and showed her the watch.

Her sister asked where on earth she had found it, and, when told, expressed utter disbelief as she had not been in his study so it could not possibly have been in there. Guessing that her husband had found it and had done this to teach her careless sister a lesson, Mayer put it back and told her not to say anything.

On her husband's return home Mayer told him that her sister had mislaid her watch and they had searched for it in vain, but without mentioning that she had found it. In reply he said that after she had gone to work he had found it lying in the bathroom and had decided to hide it in the closet in his study to teach her sister a lesson, something that neither Mayer nor her sister could possibly have known. He then went to fetch it. Mayer summed up her experience by saying "I didn't decide to walk into my husband's study – it felt more like I was being walked somehow by the experience."

These descriptions by her four intuitives of their transition from the everyday state of mind to the intuitive, plus her own experience, were interwoven with reading the voluminous research literature generated by the Society for Psychical Research (founded 1882) and American Society for Psychical Research (founded 1884) together with more recent organisations such as the Parapsychology Association, the Institute of Noetic Sciences, and the Society for Scientific Exploration. She also arranged interviews with leading researchers across the spectrum of parapsychology to help sort the pseudoscientific psi chaff from scientific psi substance. She considered that she had found real substance in the following four lines of inquiry.

Remote viewing

In the 1960s America heard that Russia was developing remote viewing, or clairvoyant, expertise for military purposes, and, in response, poured money into a CIA initiated research programme called Stargate to develop its own experts in remote detection of Soviet military projects. Harold Puthoff, physicist, founder and director of what was called the Stargate Project that ran from 1972 to 1995, took Mayer through its extensive research programme and findings. The two most famous remote viewers were Pat Price, an ex-policeman, and Joe McMoneagle, US Army Intelligence, who, given only geographical coordinates, often provided astonishingly accurate descriptions of military installations confirmed later by satellite photography. But they could do more than just observe as if from above. They could 'enter' the installations and 'see' what was going on. For example, in late 1979 McMoneagle 'entered' a massive building in northern Russia and described two huge hulls being built to create a new, twin hulled, submarine. This was met with complete disbelief as all submarines from the very beginning were single hulled but, in January, 1980, the twin hulled Typhoon class submarine was launched from that site for sea trials (McMoneagle, 1993. See also Tart, Puthoff & Targ. 2002)

Effect of psi intention

Mayer reviewed the numerous studies on psi healing as in spiritual healing, qigong, Johrei and energy healing, on everything from affecting the rate of enzyme activity, cell multiplication, cancer cell inhibition, seed germination, plant growth, wound repair, recovery from surgery, and relief of pain. Again, she interviewed leading researchers such as Larry Dossey MD, Mitchell Krucoff MD, and Dr Wayne Jonas. She found that American studies on human illness using large numbers of intercessory healers sending healing intention to people identified by name only in large trials showed mixed results as outside variables such local church prayers were difficult to control. On the other hand, individual case histories and smaller control group studies of patients attending healers repeatedly demonstrated symptom improvement, and sometimes clinical condition improvement greater than in control groups and often exceeding clinical prognosis. Two outstanding healers in America were husband and wife team Ambrose and Olga Worrall (Worrall & Worrall, 1965). Ambrose was a senior aeronautical engineer who felt that objective verification was important, so they submitted themselves to many investigations and repeatedly obtained beneficial results beyond chance expectation. Trials on the effects of mental intention on cell cultures, whether to increase cellular activity in normal cells, or inhibit activity as in cancer cells, had shown positive results compared with controls (see literature reviews by Jonas & Crawford, 2003, and Vernon, 2021). These findings indicated that the mindset of psi healing could exert an external effect known as psychokinesis (PK).

Ganzfeld studies

Ganzfeld (German meaning 'whole field' as in a continuum) studies involve paired participants, one acting as the receiver and one acting as the sender. To decrease sensory input noise in receivers compared to possible telepathic signals from senders, the receivers relax in a comfortable chair, with translucent ping pong halves over their eyes, with a lamp transmitting a mild red light and hearing quiet white noise through headphones. During the trial they report whatever images and thoughts come to mind. Senders focus on sending randomly chosen target images to the receivers. After the trial the receivers are shown the images and rank them according to how closely they match their description. These are then assessed by independent judges. Each trial consists of the target image and three decoys. Professors William Braud, Adrian Parker and the late Charles Honorton, developed the technique, including computerised autoganzfeld that removed any criticism of subjective bias in target selection. Statistical battle over the interpretation of Ganzfeld meta-analyses has been fierce, but has come down firmly in favour of a psi interpretation. A trial involving twenty highly artistic and creative students from the Juilliard School in New York, found an overall 50% average hit rate compared with 25% chance expectation, and eight music students scored an astonishing 75% hit rate (Schiltz and Honorton, 1992).

Presentiment

To test whether a soon-to-be-experienced event could affect a person before it was experienced, recordings of electrical skin conductance using conductors attached to fingers (anticipation, conscious or subconscious, increases sweat production, reducing resistance) and EEG recording of brainwaves, have been employed to detect whether any changes characteristic of increased anticipation occurred before the event itself. The participant either receives a signal on the monitor, or can voluntarily press a button ten seconds before a random image occurs on the screen. This could be either of a strong emotional nature, such as a sexual or violent picture, or a neutral image such as a green field. Other trials have used the stimulus of either a sudden sound or electric shock or no shock ten seconds later. The majority of trials have shown a rise in subconscious anticipation before experiencing the eventual shock, compared with no anticipatory change if emotionally neutral. This rise in consciously unaware anticipation of a shock to come commenced during the ten-second period before the computer randomly chose the event some 2 milliseconds before it would occur (Radin, 2006, Mossbridge, Tressoldi & Utts, 2012).

Dr Mayer's conclusion

Dr Mayer concluded that her findings from the research literature on parapsychology, together with her experiences with the four intuitives, her own unexpected experience concerning her sister's watch, plus the hundreds of ESP experiences reported by her colleagues, and her interviews with leading researchers in parapsychology, provided mutually supportive grounds for stating that the psi phenomena of ESP and PK are a fact beyond all reasonable doubt. Denying their occurrence, as she would have done without hesitation before the harp experience, does not alter the fact of their occurrence.

She found that in clairvoyance, or remote viewing, the distance between the person or object to be detected, and the person doing the detecting, is an irrelevant factor. This anomalous finding seems to apply equally well to claims concerning telepathy and intuitive readings. There appears to be no loss of signal strength and no degradation of signal information. Experiments that included electromagnetic shielding of rooms containing senders or receivers found no difference in the percentage of hit rates compared with non-shielded trials. Intervening buildings, hills, mountains, and deserts make no difference. Nor, in intuitive readings, does the number of people with the same name as the client who happen to live in the area between them, nor the sheer number of intervening brains and minds. It is as if there is only the object or the person to be intuitively detected, and the intuitive doing the detecting.

In summary

1. What is known as extrasensory perception, or ESP (also called 'anomalous cognition') of objects and people when beyond sensory detection is a fact.
2. The distance between a telepathist or remote viewer and the person or object being contacted is not a relevant factor; nor is the presence of intervening minds, or geographical features.
3. 'Direct knowing' is related to a particular state of mind experienced as different in kind from everyday consciousness.
4. Directed mental intention when in this state of mind can measurably affect the metabolism of other living systems.
5. Experiments have demonstrated that events yet-to-be-experienced can exert a subconscious, anticipatory influence on the present.

The problem for mainstream scientific acceptance

As discussed by Mayer, in science an anomaly is a deviation or departure from the range of events considered possible within the current scientific paradigm. In most cases current theory can be revised to accommodate such unexpected findings into the main canon of accepted occurrences. If the claimed anomaly runs absolutely counter to prevailing opinion as to whether it's possible, it is rejected, often correctly, as error. But if its existence becomes backed by experimental evidence beyond reasonable refutation, it acts as an intellectual catalyst and, as Kuhn (1962) interpreted the progress of scientific thought, a new paradigm of scientific understanding is created. This new paradigm integrates the former anomaly, or anomalies, with the already known within a new explanatory framework. The previously 'impossible' anomaly becomes the cornerstone of a new understanding. The history of the evolution of scientific understanding from classical physics to relativity and quantum mechanics, is punctuated by paradigmatic changes of perspective as ongoing research, especially when using new instrumental technologies results in new anomalous findings at odds with explanations based upon the current paradigm.

Psi and Science

Despite the findings of experimental parapsychology and the thousands of well attested cases of personal experiences during which new information was acquired about something, or someone, not accountable by the circumstances at the time (see Rhine Feather & Schmicker, 2005), the claim that this data is real has remained an anomaly too extreme for acceptance within mainstream science, including mainstream psychology and related neurosciences. The claimed subject matter of parapsychology does not even exist. The claim that telepathy, clairvoyance, remote viewing of objects, intuitive perception of someone's mind, premonition, precognition and post cognition are genuine psi phenomena supported by empirical findings is flatly rejected as impossible. So-called poltergeist activity just cannot happen. As far as mainstream science is concerned, 'ESP' stands for 'Error Some Place' and Psi as 'Pointless Scientific Inquiry'. This was Dr Mayer's belief prior to Major McCoy's perception of where the stolen harp was hidden.

Public science and private opinion

Although this is the public position of the mainstream sciences as presented to the general public, implying that 'all we highly qualified scientists are agreed on this', as Mayer soon discovered, it is very far from being the whole picture. Many scientists from across the scientific spectrum, including some of recognised eminence up to Nobel prize level in their field of expertise, have accepted the anecdotal and empirical evidence for psi phenomena as genuine. For example, the late Freeman John Dyson, a theoretical physicist and mathematician of world repute and emeritus professor of physics at the Institute for Advanced Study, Princeton, agreed to write the foreword to Dr Mayer's book. He said that he was certain that ESP is a genuine phenomenon, but not easily detectable in laboratory trials because in real life it is usually activated by moments of urgent emotional need. He went on to say, "One of my grandmothers was a notorious and successful faith healer, and one of my cousins was, for many years, editor of the *Journal for the Society for Psychical Research*". Both, he said, were "very intelligent and well-educated ladies and no fools." This particular cousin was Renée Haynes, granddaughter of Thomas Huxley and close friend of Arthur Koestler and Brian Inglis. Besides being the editor of the Journal of the Society for Psychical Research (SPR) for many years, she also wrote two books on ESP (Haynes, 1961, 1976). To date, the presidents of the SPR have included physicists, astronomers, mathematicians, philosophers, classicists, psychologists, physiologists and biologists. Three Presidents, Charles Richet, physiologist, Robert John Strutt (Lord Rayleigh), physicist, and Henri Bergson, literature, were Nobel Prize winners (See Appendices).

The majority of scientists tend to keep any belief in ESP/Psi to themselves, as they do not wish to run the risk of losing the respect of their unyielding peers and, possibly, their career prospects. Dr Daryl Bem, then professor of social psychology, Cornell University, referred Mayer to a survey of some 1,100 USA college professors as to their personal belief concerning psi. Did they think that it was an established fact, or a likely possibility? Or did they think that psi was an unlikely possibility or not possible. Of those who answered 'Yes' to one or other of the first two options, 55% were natural scientists, 66% were social scientists, 66% were in the arts and humanities, and 77% were educationalists. Of the psychologists who responded 34% expressed belief in one or other of the first two options, while 34% held the opposite view.

Noting that magicians who, knowing all the tricks of the trade, have exposed hundreds of so-called mediums and psychics as frauds, Dr Mayer wondered whether they were just as convinced as the sceptical psychologists that psi does not exist. To her complete surprise a survey found that between around 78- 84% of magicians believed that ESP was a genuine phenomenon (Parker, 2003).

Initial psi experience - fear and rejection

When Dr John B. Rhine, Director of the Parapsychology Laboratory, Duke University, published his ESP research findings in his first two books (Rhine 1934, Rhine, Pratt *et al.*, 1940), they became world news. He received an unexpected flood of letters from people who, in recounting their apparently telepathic, apparitional, or clairvoyant experiences, were desperate to know if they were going mad and asking if he could please help them. Many had never told anyone for fear of being mocked. All had tried to find a sensible, rational, explanation, and it was their failure to do so that caused their fear.

His wife, Dr Louisa Rhine, filed over 15,000 of such accounts and eventually sorted and published several hundred of them (Rhine 1961, 1967, 1981). She noted that the majority of correspondents said that at the time of the occurrence they did not believe in ESP phenomena. A similar response is common to those experiencing poltergeist phenomena (Gauld & Cornell, 1979). The normal reaction is a determined search for an explanation in terms of natural causes and chance coincidence. When the activity continues beyond such possible explanations, the next search is to try to find those suspected of tomfoolery and trickery. Like Mayer, most people want a normal, everyday reason, and expect to find it if only they look carefully enough. This initial rejection of any ESP/Psi based explanation is important, as it refutes the claim that such accounts can always be laid at the door of credulous gullibility and misguided belief in ESP/Psi phenomena.

Figure and ground comment

A central concept in gestalt psychology is our attempt to resolve ambiguity, whether of sight, sound, smell, taste or circumstance so that it makes sense within our understanding of the ways of the world. Resolving an ambiguity by choosing interpretation A, instead of interpretation B, involves a change of our previous awareness of B as an alternative option to a sudden, complete, non-awareness of B at the moment of choice, and vice versa. Gestalt defines this decisional non awareness in terms of figure and ground, or foreground and background. Rubin's vase (figure 3) is a well-known example where you can see either a white central vase profile within a black background OR two white faced profiles facing each other separated by a black space. You can flip from one to the other, but cannot see both at the same time.

Rubin's vase is a useful analogy concerning the debate on parapsychology. People of equal intelligence, qualifications, and belief in the scientific method resolve the debate in accordance with their prior A based belief, or prior B based belief, with regard to what is possible and what is not possible. It remains polarised between those who, using the vase analogy, see the twin profiles symbolising rejection of ESP/Psi, and those who see the central vase as symbolising acceptance of ESP/Psi. This conceptual blindness whereby choice A vanishes B, and choice B vanishes A, means that proponents of either view just talk past each other. They use the same language and possess the same skills of reasoning, but their polarised interpretation, based upon their prior belief, determines their argument.

Once that stance has been made public and you become identified with it, it becomes far more difficult to change from, say, sceptical twin profile A to psi acceptance vase B, as you risk losing credibility in the eyes of your sceptical colleagues. It is also much easier to move from B to A as it carries the reward of admission into your sceptical, hard headed, peer group.

Is there possible resolution?

For parapsychology, is there a way of resolving these A or B differences into a greater whole of (AB) integrated into a new C? Is there the possibility of a paradigmatic shift by way of analogy with figure 3, in which the right-hand, two-dimensional profiles versus vase become absorbed into an inclusive, three dimensional, left hand whole?

Two dimensional either/   Three dimensional
or profiles   inclusive whole

Figure 3. Towards an inclusive paradigm

The search for answers – the background

Fully aware that mainstream scientific thought rejected all such claims as impossible in principle, so impossible in practice, Mayer felt that her next step was to search for a theory that could accommodate these findings and provide grounds for a new scientific paradigm in which psi would be an anomaly no more. In late 1995 she heard a taped lecture on parapsychology given by the late Robert G Jahn. It was one of a series of lectures recorded by the Centre for Frontier Sciences, Temple University, Philadelphia. Professor Jahn, then Dean of the School of Engineering and Applied Science, Princeton University, was a world expert in the field of aeronautical sciences and rocket propulsion.

In 1977 one of his final year students wanted to do her dissertation on whether mental intention could affect external physical processes. Feeling very sceptical, but finding that he could not persuade her to choose a more orthodox engineering topic, he designed a random binary number generator whereby a cursor placed an advancing series of dots across a computer screen from left to right that deviated at random either side of the horizontal mean with no overall bias towards '1's above the line or 'O's below the line. Left on its own it did just that but, to Jahn's surprise, when subject to mental intention to track either above, or below the mean, there was a slight bias over many runs that eventually reached statistical significance as the number of runs mounted in favour of the intended deviation. In 1979, with his psychologist colleague Dr Brenda Dunne, he set up the Princeton Engineering Anomalies Research (PEAR) laboratory in the basement of the university, and, over the next 25 years thousands of such experiments followed, resulting in a large body of statistical research findings that, they felt, confirmed the findings of that initial student. The odds against chance were one billion to one (10^9). Some participants were found to be more effective than others, providing further confirmation that something more than chance was involved. It was found that the more successful participants were those who just expected the cursor line to deviate above or below the line rather than trying to exert willpower.

Remote viewing

A second line of Jahn's research involved remote viewing in which the agent, as 'sender', visited a randomly chosen scene and recorded its visual topography on a standard check sheet together with photographs. At the same time the 'percipient' or 'receiver', who might be many miles away and was ignorant of the chosen site, noted down their inner 'perceptions' on the same standardised check sheet plus any other comments or sketches. The check sheets were then digitized and their degree of concordance scored numerically. The results from hundreds of these experiments were even more successful than the random binary number generator trials, with odds estimated at one hundred billion to one (10^{11}) against chance as the agent responsible.

When Mayer published a paper (Mayer, 1996) that included reference to their findings as presented in their 1987 book *Margins of Reality: The role of consciousness in the physical world*, she sent a copy to Jahn and Dunne. In reply they invited her to lecture at an interdisciplinary meeting of the International Consciousness Research Laboratory (ICRL) and she then joined them in looking for an explanation of ESP/Psi.

Psi and quantum theory

Combining their respective professional expertise Jahn, Dunne and Mayer proposed a tentative model of mind-to-mind communication and mind to matter interaction illustrated by a quadrant box with the left-hand quadrant pair headed as 'mind' and the right-hand quadrant pair headed as 'matter' (figure 4).

MIND	MATTER
TANGIBLE CONSCIOUS DYNAMICS Everyday waking experiences of self, relationships, time, getting things done	TANGIBLE DYNAMICS Everyday world of objects, space, time, cause and effect
NON-CONSCIOUS DYNAMICS Dreams, intuitions, subconscious awareness, dissolving of time and space Psi – ESP/PK	INTANGIBLE DYNAMICS Quantum world of probabilities, entanglement, non-locality

Figure 4. Adapted from *Extraordinary Knowing* (Mayer, 2007)

The upper left and right quadrant pair represents what they termed as the tangible dynamics of our everyday conscious mind and the tangible dynamics of the everyday world 'out there'. The two tangibles, conscious mind and matter, are separate entities that interact through our bodily senses and our purposeful activity in a reality of space, time, objects, and cause and effect. This is represented by the solid line that separates them.

The lower left-hand quadrant represents what they term as the intangible, non-conscious, dynamics of mind. This is the home of dreams, implicit memory and associative emotional networks based upon past experiences and, they proposed, the source of ESP/Psi. In this non-conscious dynamic, time, cause and effect do not follow such linear rules. It is not governed by the thought processes of everyday life but often intrudes into everyday consciousness in apparently illogical ways, causing us to think, or do, the unexpected. Often, in retrospect, we realise that the apparently irrational 'gut' decision was the right decision.

The lower right-hand quadrant represents the intangible dynamics of the atomic to subatomic world of quantum mechanics. Here, the everyday world of classical physics, of a before and an after, of cause and effect, dissolves into probabilities of occurring or not occurring without cause. Locality, in the sense of the 'hereness and thereness' that we take for granted, dissolves into a nonlocality of everywhere yet nowhere. Particles, once entangled with opposite spins, thus maintaining quantum parity, remain mutually connected even when, as measured by our everyday reality, they are moving away from each other at speeds close to the speed of light. If particle A has its clockwise spin reversed, the anticlockwise spin of particle B reverses simultaneously, thus preserving quantum parity. Such instant simultaneity of paired action is not possible in the upper right hand quadrant world as distance apart and the speed of light as the limiting factor in transmitting information from A to B are the determining factors. In our everyday world there is always a time lag, but, in the quantum relationship of mutual particle entanglement, time and space are irrelevant.

Quantum reality is so contrary to our everyday reality that analogies taken from everyday life make little sense and its properties are best modelled in terms of equations. Non-conscious dynamics also is contrary to everyday rational thinking. While the different realities of the upper and lower quadrant pairs exist, the cause-and-effect properties of the upper pair cannot be used to predict the properties and behaviour of the lower pair. In fact, the causal properties of the upper pair deny the very possibility of their lower quadrant properties. Such properties, including ESP/PK phenomena, are completely unexplainable in upper quadrant logic, so any claim that they have intruded into the upper quadrant world of everyday mind and everyday matter is met with denial.

The three authors propose that at the interface between the upper and lower quadrants, a transformation occurs between intangible consciousness to tangible consciousness and intangible matter to tangible matter. For an ESP event to occur (telepathy, clairvoyance, premonition) it is transformed from nonconscious to direct conscious perception. For a PK effect to occur, the PK intention can be visualised as passing from the unconscious dynamic into the quantum dynamic to bias the collapse of quantum indeterminacy into our cause-and-effect reality. For example, to achieving the desired PK effect of accelerating seed germination or cell division, or inhibiting cancer cell proliferation (represented by the dotted lines).

Psi-quantum interaction

From the viewpoint of mainstream science and everyday experience, the left and right upper quadrant pair of subjective mind and objective matter remain completely separate from each other on either side of the vertical dividing line. However, based upon their belief that the hypothesis of psi is supported by proven psi phenomena, Jahn, Dunne and Mayer felt that there must be some degree of mind/matter interaction across the lower vertical divide. They argued that as ESP/PK phenomena are not explainable by the tangible properties of the upper pair, the answer must lie in the intangible properties of the lower pair. In his 2006 book *Entangled Minds: Extrasensory Experiences in a Quantum Reality*, Dr Dean Radin, Chief Scientist at the Institute of Noetic Sciences (IONS), Petaluma, CA., argues along very similar lines.

To Jahn and Dunne, the findings from their research clearly indicated that the faculty of psi is present in all of us at non conscious level. As with all human abilities, some people are far more psi sensitive and responsive than others. True intuitives have learned how to slip into the mindset of 'direct knowing' whether of people or objects. In 'direct knowing' distance and time is not a factor. The best Stargate viewers such as McMoneagle said that once given the coordinates they did not 'go' anywhere from where they actually were. They somehow 'went inside' as if they, and the site, were as one. Harold McCoy and Dr Mayer's four main intuitives described their experiences in very similar terms, and Mayer had a similar experience when she found the watch.

'Direct knowing' and brain-mind correlation

Whatever the answer, it should be possible to find a correlation between the altered mental state of 'direct knowing' and correlated brain activity using the techniques of brain scanning. Newberg and D'Aquili (2001) used such techniques with Buddhist meditators and Franciscan nuns when engaged in deep meditation or prayer. In their case, as they became absorbed in deep meditation and deep meditative prayer, there was reduced activity in the areas of the brain concerned with awareness of their body, their surroundings, and their sense of time. As they entered the state of mind in which they felt that they had become 'as one' with the universe or, for the nuns, with the Presence of God, conscious awareness of this world disappeared.

In his 2015 book *Psychic Phenomena and the Brain: Exploring the Neurophysiology of Psi*, neurophysiologist Bryan William has further confirmed this finding, showing that there is increasing EEG and brain scanning evidence that 'direct knowing' is a particular state of altered consciousness that has its own neurological correlate.

When, for example, intuitives enter the ESP state of 'direct knowing' this automatically reduces the neural correlate related to the mental "noise" of sensory based input and related attention, rather like turning down a noisy television set to the point where you become aware of a quiet radio programme playing in the background. This change in ESP/sensory signal to noise ratio (S/N) in favour of ESP seems to amplify the ESP signal reciprocally and facilitate entry of 'direct knowing' into consciousness.

If Jahn, Dunne, Mayer and many other investigators are correct, the psi faculty is present in all of us as a background information channel. Clinical psychologist James Carpenter (2012) has argued that ESP predates the senses in being the earliest form of information gathering about our environment. As in the title of his 2012 book *First-Sight: ESP and Parapsychology in Everyday Life*, he has termed this primary, pre-sensory, process 'First Sight', in contrast to the implications of the term 'Second Sight', traditionally attributed to sensitives of Scottish descent as an inherited psychic ability.

The late psychologist Lawrence Le Shan (1980, 2009) referred to this level of direct knowing as 'Clairvoyant Reality'. Mayer has termed it 'Extraordinary Knowing' or 'Intuitive Intelligence'. At the start of her first reading with Dr Mayer, Deb Mangulus actually describes the very moment of transition from everyday sensory reality to the inner reality of 'direct knowing' when she says, "I'll take a few seconds to be sure *it is you I am seeing*" (my italics). Once she was *seeing* she then *knew*, what neither she, nor anyone, could possibly have known in sensory reality about a person who, some 2,700 miles away at the other end of the telephone, just says 'My name is Elizabeth'.

A new paradigm for psychology?

Harold McCoy's location of the stolen harp and Mayer's first reading with Deb Mangulus in which she described her change from her everyday mind to her 'direct knowing' mind really happened. They are facts, not errors of gullible interpretation. Such well attested accounts are backed by findings from parapsychology research. This being so, surely the most reasonable position to adopt is to accept that 'direct knowing' actually occurs. Denial is not an appropriate response to a well proven, persistent, anomaly. By analogy with Rubin's three-dimensional vase, what is needed is a new paradigm of psychology that recognises psi as a genuine property of mind. The various ways that psi presents itself can then become legitimate areas of inquiry within mainstream psychology.

Implications for physics

Psychology, by definition, is the study of the psyche, consisting of mental qualia not physical quanta. Acceptance of psi as a function of mind has no relevance to what the physical sciences discover about the physical universe. It would not undermine scientific findings or theories about the material universe. They can offer no explanation for the existence of mental phenomena because it does not lie within the explanatory framework of physics. In the physical world, modelled in terms of formulae, laws and equations, mental reality has not been found. It exists as its own reality and remains stubbornly different in kind. But, despite this, in some unknowable way, mentality can interact with the physical world.

Conclusion

If psi and psi phenomena were formally recognised as genuine psychological functions, the result would be the creation of a science of the whole mind. A new psychological paradigm. A three-dimensional vase. Mayer's 'Extraordinary Knowing' would be recognised as a category of 'direct knowing' that is other than the ordinary knowing as gained through the senses. Psi could then be explored as a genuine phenomenon in its own right including, for example, what really happens when an intuitive says to his or her, faraway client 'I'll take a few seconds to be sure *it is you I am seeing*', and it really is you who is being *'seen'* and no one else.

Note: Dr Mayer had just finished the text of her book before dying in her sleep at her parents' home in Hanover, N.H., on New Year's Day, 2005, of complications from intestinal scleroderma, a rare disease that she had suffered from for more than 15 years. The end note references and index were completed by Meg and Byrdie Renik, and Pamela and Rebecca Mayer.[7]

9

Discussion

The main purpose of this book has been to present evidence that the 'psi mind' is able to interact with the external world. This includes exerting an effect on other living systems, both at cellular and mental level, and on matter, as in the Toronto group's table turning and 'Eric's answering wall rapping. When in a meditative state the psi mind has been shown to have a calming effect on the local population, and descriptions of OBEs have been verified repeatedly. A stolen harp was located by map dowsing from 1800 miles away, and it seems that personal possessions can disappear and reappear somewhere else. Refusing to admit that these phenomena occur, which is the present position of mainstream science theory and psychology, does not alter the fact that they do.

The interaction of the world of our mentality, both conscious and non-conscious, and the inferred world of the physical sciences is more complex than we imagined. I say 'inferred world' because we cannot directly experience the nature of the physical world as described in the textbooks and scientific journals. We know 'of it' as theoretical knowledge only. For example, we experience 'light and colour' as our immediate reality. But 'light' is not the electromagnetic frequencies themselves, nor the retinal stimulation, nor the resulting patterns of nerve impulses in the brain centres dealing with vision. 'Light', as in the visual scene, is an emergent resultant that is not present in any of the preceding physical processes. All species live in the immediacy of experiential reality, but we are the only species that knows there are two realities:

A. An inferred physical reality. This is the reality that forms the physical universe, including our bodies and brains. It is quantitative in nature, and its properties can be summarised in laws and equations.
B. Experiential reality. This is the mental reality of immediate experiencing, consciousness, and inward imagining. It is qualitative in nature only, so is not bound by laws and equations as it has no basic units. It is the mentality possessed by all creatures that have a brain.

Brain and mind

Despite the incredible advances in the neurosciences we still have no idea what it is about brain activity, a bioelectrical activity going on inside our heads that we cannot consciously detect and experience, that results in a mental reality that we do experience. As mental beings our nature is qualitative in nature only, by that I mean that there are no physical units of mental energy, so we are not constrained by the physical properties of the brain. Yet despite brain and mind being so different in kind, one physical and the other mental, so neither should have any effect on the other as they have no property in common, by some exception to the rules the evidence shows that they can and do. In our everyday state of mind we exert a directional control of our brain, and, through the brain, of our daily physical activity, and the evidence presented in this book indicates that when we are in our psi state of mind, we can influence the external world, both in having an intended result, and sometimes completely unintentionally.

Healing and the non-placebo studies

The best evidence for this effect comes from the numerous non-placebo studies where seeds, cells and tissues exposed to healing intention have demonstrated an increase in metabolic activity compared with controls. A greater percentage of seeds germinate, seedlings grow more quickly, tissue cells divide more frequently, and tissues heal more quickly. This implies that the mind of the psi healer is having a direct, stimulatory, effect on the enzyme systems that control metabolism. Conversely, when the intention is to inhibit unwanted cell activity, cancer cells grow more slowly and have shorter life spans, and, in a dramatic series of experiments, mice injected with a normally fatal dose of cancer cells have lived, whereas those mice that did not receive healing died. Not only that, but mice that have received injections of immunity cells taken from those same mice, have remained immune to cancer cell injection.

The implications of these non-placebo findings for orthodox medical practice are considerable. Whereas the symptom relief experienced by patients on receiving psi healing is usually attributed to placebo effect only, a major contributory factor may be occurring at the site of the disease process itself, with reduction in inflammation, inhibition of pathological processes, and acceleration of tissue healing. Symptom relief, which is experienced as mental relief, also has a positive effect on brain activity, resulting in an increase in natural endorphins to sustain relief from pain and discomfort, and a reduction in stress hormones, thus enhancing the effectiveness of the body's own healing processes.

The results of EEG studies on healers and healees imply that they can enter into a mentally united relationship during the healing session. When healers enter the psi healing mindset their brain wave frequencies, and the amplitude of certain frequencies, stabilise into a recognisable frequency profile when shown on a monitor screen. During a healing session the brainwave profiles of the healee, that initially varies widely from the healer's profiles, comes into close synchrony with the profile of the healer, as if entrained by the steady state of the healer's mind and brain. After the session is over, the healee's brainwave profiles return towards their normal activity as everyday life is picked up again.

This is what the research evidence on the effects of psi healing, almost unknown in the medical world, and maybe still largely unknown even within the world of healing, has shown. At present, psi healing is classed as a complementary therapy, and any symptom relief or other improvement is considered in terms of placebo effect only. This is why orthodox medicine has not felt the need to investigate further, even when unexpected reduction in signs and symptoms, and sometimes even cure, is reported. In consequence, these non-placebo findings have not been looked for or taken into clinical account but, hopefully, their implications will be explored. For a thorough, up-to-date, research-based review of the enormous therapeutic contribution that psi healing can make in the treatment of many conditions I can recommend healer Sandy Edward's new book *Spiritual Healing in Hospitals and Clinics: Scientific Evidence that Energy Medicine promotes speedy recovery and positive outcomes* (2021).

The meditation studies

Although the many studies of the effects of Group Transcendental Meditation (TM-Sidhi) on the surrounding population do not fall into the traditional heading of non-placebo studies, they were non-placebo in effect, as the surrounding population was unaware of their existence. The positive influence of TM-Sidhi on community well-being has been measured in the coincident reduction in crime rates that have acted as an objective indicator, and Quality of Life surveys have found that people felt happier and more relaxed. I have suggested that practitioners of TM-Sidhi leave their everyday mind and enter into a psi state of mind, and it is when in that psi state that they affect other people. In principle, this would apply to the practitioners of any meditation system, whether practiced as a group or individually, so having a calming influence on the surrounding neighbourhood. Whether the external mental effect of psi is mediated through a Universal Field of Consciousness in which we are all immersed, remains unknown. The sociological evidence indicates that meditation affects the everyday state of mind of other people at a subconscious level, having a more pervasive effect when they are feeling relaxed and resting, and during sleep.

This seems to be an appropriate point in this discussion on meditation to relate the following story as told to me during a conference by another conference member. She was a social worker who practiced TM-Sidhi and knew the research literature. She lived close to the local prison and knew the prison governor as a friend. She had told him about the TM-Sidhi research and had asked him if he would be willing to try a very unofficial experiment. For a given period of a few days she, together with some TM-Sidhi practicing friends, would meet at her house for twice daily group TM-Sidhi meditation. With no one else in the prison knowing about this, the governor would note from the morning reports and daily discussions with staff if there was any change in prisoner violence, attitude to staff, and overall prison atmosphere. Well, it seems that there was. Rather surprised and relieved staff reported fewer instances of violence, less shouting and swearing, less hostility, more good humour, and a more generally relaxed atmosphere during that same period. Unfortunately, as it was just an informal experiment, it was never written up. It could have been coincidence and, of course, the governor was looking for any changes, so could have over interpreted what he was being told. Follow up studies along similar lines could either confirm whether those unofficial findings were valid or a one-off anomaly.

Out-of-Body Observations (OBOs)

Hundreds of OBOs that have occurred during an OBE have now been verified, thus demonstrating that they were not a hallucinatory dream. Based upon Professor Jimo Borjigin's experimental findings – that during the process of dying, each rat brain, including those that were anaesthetised, unexpectedly exhibited a brief period of intense brainwave activity that normally correlated with consciousness – I have proposed that OBEs and their accompanying OBOs occur during a similar period in some patients when anaesthetised as well when someone has fainted and is unconscious. As the EEGs of patients are rarely monitored during most operations, including during cardiac resuscitation, there would be no outward sign that a conscious OBE had occurred with an accompanying OBO. A common feature of these OBOs is that they were observed as if from above, or alongside those present. While subjective verifications by others could be challenged as errors in remembering where they were at that time, two particular verifications seem irrefutable. One was of the patient who correctly remembered seeing a 12-digit number stamped on the top of a tall cardiac monitor (for example - 2053691324806) and the other was of the patient who remembered seeing a silver dime on one corner of a cardiac monitor. Both of these observations were factually verified.

This implies that during an OBE, people are conscious of their mental whereabouts in relationship to what they are seeing and where other people are. I have proposed that as there is no sensory input from the anaesthetised sensory nervous system, the everyday state of mind is not operating, and it is the psi mind that is consciously observing the scene. The memory is laid down and is available to the everyday mind on reawakening.

Psi mind effects on matter

If the effects of psi healing, and the social effects of group meditation, may be difficult to accept as they lie so FAR outside the daily norm, at least the phenomena occur between living systems, so there is the possibility of an explanation. But the claim that mind can affect inanimate matter may well be a step too far, as there seems to be no possibility of an explanation. Matter obeys the laws and equations of physics, as expressed in Newton's Laws and the attraction of gravity on mass, without exception.

The problem is that there are exceptions. The answering raps and table movements that occurred when the eight members of the Toronto Society for Psychical Research met to hold a session with 'Philip', were filmed twice and televised once. They were also seen by many independent observers who testified to their occurrence. 'Philip' suddenly, and unexpectedly, appeared as a mentally created entity that 'inhabited' a table during the group sessions, answering questions by raps and displaying semi-autonomous table moving behaviour that the group often could not predict. While they tried to keep their hands on the table they lost touch as the table went this way and that. In between sessions it was just an ordinary table. The significant difference concerning the state of the table was that, as Margaret Sparrow described it: "When Philip was there – even if there was no movement or rapping – the table had a feeling of aliveness, perhaps of vibration, which seemed to be quite different from its feel under normal circumstances". The table had somehow become 'mentalised', but only when the members were in 'Philip' session. In between, it was just an ordinary wooden table that obeyed the laws of physics.

I have suggested that 'Philip' was created during the periods when the group had temporarily transitioned into a psi state of mind in which they believed that 'Philip' would be present within the table. I have very, very, tentatively suggested that 'Philip' somehow interacted with the quantum processes that create the properties of mass to temporarily nullify Newton's Laws of Motion with regard to mass inertia and the effect of gravity on mass

The evidence for the existence of 'Eric', the responsive wall rapper who 'lived' with the Andrews family for 8 weeks in 1974, is also beyond dispute. Acoustic analysis of 'Eric's' raps compared with knuckle and other forms of applied taps demonstrated beyond doubt that the waveform of 'his' raps was very different from that of applied taps. They seemed to be somehow generated within the wall or bedhead, rising in amplitude until released as a rap sound. 'Eric' could also, apparently of his own will, generate loud vibratory bangs in the wall that could be heard in the street. In some way he seemed to be related to twelve-year-old Theresa, as her presence in the bedroom that she shared with Maria seemed to be necessary at the beginning. Why 'Eric', as 'he' called himself, came into existence one evening when Theresa and Maria were quietly chatting, and why he faded away 8 weeks later remains unknown. 'His' appearance falls under the general healing of poltergeist phenomena, where the theory is that intense, suppressed emotions are released as external phenomena. But, as far as Dr Barrie Colvin, who investigated the case, could see, this did not apply to quiet Theresa; but we have no idea of family relationships when he was not there.

The reason that both of these cases have been presented is that the evidence for their occurrence is beyond reasonable dispute. Like the other cases covered in previous chapters, they fall well outside what mainstream science theory and psychology deems possible, but they happened despite this, so must be taken into account when theorising about the nature of mentality.

Personal possessions

If the other subjects covered in this book fall well outside what mainstream theory deems possible, the claim that small, physical possessions such as keys, wallets, or whatever, could disappear, reappear, or be replaced by something else, presents a whole new level of impossibility. What is meant by 'disappear' and 'reappear' is that the object dematerialised out of physical existence, causing much frustration and distress, and re-materialised again back into physical existence, causing relief mixed with bewilderment, or it never rematerialized to the owner, but materialised to someone else as an unknown object for which there was no explanation. All this for no apparent cause.

There is an oft quoted saying that 'A man convinced against his will, is of the same opinion still', and this surely applied to me when I first read about such claimed experiences in Barrington's book. There MUST be a normal explanation because they just could not dematerialise or re-materialise. They were mislaid, or dropped without knowing, or someone else had picked them up, and then forgotten that they had, or someone was playing a prank, but it had gone too far so they stayed quiet. Or they were making it up to see how gullible other people were. Or something!

But when I talked to Barrington about jotts before reviewing her book, she assured me that with her suspicious legal mind very much intact, she had interviewed the people and examined the circumstances of each of the 160 cases quoted in her book. Dr Jinks, as an academic psychologist, has obviously taken the same line regarding the 385 cases presented in his book, so we have some 545 cases of jotts overall by the time both books were published, and presumably many more have been gathered by Jinks now. I should add that the more usual name for objects, which behave so strangely, is 'apports'.

I have included these cases of what has been termed 'jotting' because they are verified observations and must, somehow, relate to the relationship between the human mind and physical reality. The psi hypothesis doesn't seem to apply here, because, as far as can be judged, every jott experient was very much in their everyday state of mind and even more so when frantically looking for what has disappeared, or staring in disbelief at its return, or its even more baffling replacement. Both investigators have

DISCUSSION

put forward a tentative mind/physical world relationship hypothesis as to how jotts may happen, and I have suggested that maybe it is at a more fundamental level than the psi mind.

Dr Mayer's inquiry into psi

I have included a review of her findings across psi phenomena as they provide a wider clinical and research perspective, and include an interesting theory as to how psi at subconscious level may influence the everyday state of mind, and, through its possible effects at quantum level, manifest itself in everyday reality. Of all the myriad examples of psi mind activity, Major Harold McCoy's location of where the harp was hidden through clairvoyant map dowsing is THE example of the psi mind in action beyond any possibility of a non-psi explanation. If you accept Mayer's account as occurring as described, then you have to accept that psi phenomena are genuine. If you don't accept that it occurred as claimed, then the only recourse open to you is to question the veracity of those involved, which seems a rather drastic step to take. Mayer's four intuitives offer a valuable insight into the necessity of moving from the everyday mind into the psi mind before commencing a reading. Unless they have entered the psi mindset the intuitives are unable to 'know' their client.

The two-mind hypothesis

This is not offered as some kind of explanation because, as yet, we have no explanation. We haven't even an explanation for the everyday state of mind, and this fact seems repeatedly to be overlooked by neuroscientists trying to 'explain' psychology in terms of neurology, and sceptics rejecting psi. What this hypothesis is proposing is that there is a particular class of phenomena for which mainstream science and psychology can offer no explanation and therefore rejects, and that phenomena occur only when in the psi state of mind (jotts excepted). That such phenomena do occur is demonstrated by the scientific evidence and verified observations included in this book. They occur when people are in a different state of mind from the everyday state. In my previous book I looked at cases of ESP that can be considered as the receptive side of psi. In this book I present objective evidence that the mind, when in the psi mindset, can affect the external world. The fact that we do not know how it can do this, is not a good reason to deny that it can, and it does, and the fact that it does, requires an explanation.

Science and Psi (not science versus psi)

Although Wikipedia receives much criticism, I have always found its entries on whatever I am researching to be very helpful and informative, with one exception. That exception is that anything to do with parapsychology is dismissed by Wikipedia as a pseudoscience. The argument is that claims for the existence of psi fly in the face of the laws of science as we know it, so such claims cannot be true. Parapsychologists are wasting their time searching for a phenomenon that does not exist because it cannot exist. Like many similar sceptic websites, their message is that if someone is of a scientific turn of mind, or has scientific qualifications from BSc(Hons) to a PhD, they will automatically reject anything classed 'parapsychological' as 'pseudoscience'. Science says that it cannot happen, so it follows that it does not happen. But there are two problems with this argument. Firstly,

Discussion

if psi is a mental attribute, then it is not constrained by physical laws. Secondly, this is not the spirit in which true scientific inquiry is carried out. True scientific inquiry starts out with no limiting presuppositions, and follows where the evidence leads. In the case of psi healing for example, many true scientists, whose scientific curiosity was aroused by claims of a beneficial psi healing effect, have carried out numerous, non-placebo, controlled trials, and have accumulated a considerable body of empirical evidence demonstrating that psi healing is a genuine phenomenon.

Physicist Freeman John Dyson

As an example of one leading scientist's acceptance of psi, Dr Elizabeth Mayer's book, *Extraordinary Knowing*, carries an extended foreword by the late Freeman John Dyson, FRS (1923-2020). Freeman Dyson is described by Wikipedia as "An English-American theoretical physicist and mathematician, known for his works in quantum field theory, astrophysics, random matrices, mathematical formulation of quantum mechanics, condensed matter physics, nuclear physics, and engineering. He was Professor Emeritus, Institute for Advanced Study, Princeton, and a member of the Board of Sponsors of the Bulletin of Atomic Scientists." (retrieved 23/08/22). His foreword to Mayer's book concerns ESP, and makes for interesting reading:

> There are three possible positions that one may take concerning the evidence for ESP. First, the position of orthodox scientists, who believe that ESP does not exist. Second, the position of true believers who believe that ESP is real and can be proved to exist by scientific methods. Third, my own position, that ESP is real, as the anecdotal evidence

suggests, but cannot be tested by the clumsy tools of science. These positions also imply different views concerning the proper scope of science. If one believes, as many of my scientific colleagues believe, that the scope of science is unlimited, then science can explain everything in the universe, and ESP must either be non-existent or scientifically explainable. If one believes, as I do, that ESP exists but is scientifically untestable, one must believe that the scope of science is limited. I put forward, as a working hypothesis, that ESP is real, but belongs to a mental universe that is too fluid and evanescent to fit within the rigid protocols of controlled scientific testing. I do not claim that this hypothesis is true, I claim only that it is consistent with the evidence and worthy of consideration.

With regard to PK as a manifestation of psi we are on firmer scientific ground than ESP, as the claim is eminently testable. A PK effect either happens, or it does not happen.

The Society for Psychical Research

The Society for Psychical Research (SPR) was founded in 1882 by Cambridge academics "to examine without prejudice or prepossession, and in a scientific spirit, those faculties of man, real and proposed, which appear to be inexplicable on any generalised hypothesis." These faculties were telepathy, clairvoyance, precognition, post cognition, and psychokinesis. The SPR's records started from a formidable body of evidence already collected by many investigators, including many eminent scientists of the time, who became contributing members of the Society. The two Appendices listing the Presidents of the SPR provide a very necessary corrective to the view that scientists, by definition, reject the validity of psi phenomena. They include many eminent scientists, including two Nobel Prize physics winners, as well as eminent philosophers (including a Nobel Prize winner), psychologists, biologists and classical scholars. They were, and are, willing to stand up and publicly declare that the evidence for psi is scientifically acceptable. Not only that, but the majority of SPR Council members have been, and are, academics, and, over the same 140 years of its existence, so have a high percentage of the membership. Unlike the dismissive, and unnamed Wikipedia authors, they have followed where the evidence has led. Welsh born physicist and emeritus professor of physics, University of Cambridge, Brian David Josephson, FRS – who was awarded the Nobel Prize for Physics in 1983 for his research into superconductivity and quantum tunnelling that became known as the Josephson Effect – firmly believes that the evidence for psi phenomena is scientifically validated.

What tends to be overlooked is that scientists who have chosen to study psi phenomena have qualified in the orthodox sciences, and use the same investigative and analytical skills. It seems that the main reason why psi is still publicly rejected by mainstream science is based on an a priori assumption that it cannot be true, so editors of the main scientific journals refuse to publish evidence to the contrary for fear of losing scientific credibility with their peers. In many ways this reluctance is understandable, as psi is tainted with unscrupulous charlatans keen to profit from credulity, but this does not alter the fact that, of itself, psi has repeatedly been demonstrated, and personally experienced, as a genuine phenomenon.

Widening the discussion away from research

When reading reports of scientific studies in psi phenomena, and meta-analyses of studies with all those statistics, it is easy to feel that they have been carried out on a different planet from the one you live on, as they seem so far apart from everyday life. But, from talking to many people, especially during discussions after giving a talk, or during leisure time in conferences and study days, my impression is that psi experiences are happening all the time. But, like jotts, are often dismissed by a baffled 'must have been just one of those things, but very odd all the same'. People can, and do, sometimes slip into a psi state in which they have an ESP experience. When back in their everyday state of mind they know something unusual has happened, but just cannot account for it. If you want to read more about such unexpected ESP experiences I recommend *The Gift: The Extraordinary Experiences of Ordinary People* (2005) by psychologist Dr Sally Rhine Feather, and researcher Michael Schmicker.

The following accounts of someone having an ESP experience are selected from what people have told me. I cannot prove they are true, but, as I listened to the person telling me what happened, they rang true to me.

The aunt's missing car keys

I had been invited by a University of the Third Age group (U3A) to give a talk on telepathy, so in July 2017 some fifty U3A members and I met in a community centre one sunny afternoon. After the talk, several members described what they felt had been a telepathic experience of sudden awareness of what was happening to someone else that was later confirmed, or knew that someone was coming and they duly did. There were still hands in the air before the Chairperson called a halt for welcome tea and cakes. However, this story was very different.

One of the U3A members, who was a retired school teacher, approached me during the tea break to say that she wanted to tell me about an odd experience that had happened to her earlier in the year. It had left her feeling baffled and rather unnerved, as she had never experienced anything like it before, nor had she since. A very elderly aunt of her husband and brother-in-law had died after a short illness, and the two of them were tasked with settling her estate. She had met the aunt a couple of times but had never visited her home and knew very little about her. The aunt was unusual in that she was a real 'petrolhead' and owned a valuable classic car. One Friday evening the brothers met at the aunt's house to go through her effects, which included the car in the garage. They decided to take it for a short run to make sure that everything was in order before getting it evaluated, but were unable to find the keys which, they had assumed, would be in her large handbag. The next day they returned, rechecked her handbag in case the lining was loose, and methodically searched the house and garage from top to bottom – but to no avail. Her husband returned home in a very frustrated and exasperated mood as this made no sense because the aunt had been driving immediately before becoming ill.

Why weren't the keys in her handbag when everything else you would expect to find was there? They went to bed still puzzling over where she could have put them. On Sunday morning her husband got up first to prepare breakfast and let the dogs out. After he had gone she fell into a brief sleep, and experienced a very vivid dream in which she saw what looked like a kitchen door. The wallpaper above the lintel came down onto it but on the right-hand side it was loose, with a small vertical slit and a bulge where it touched the lintel. She woke up certain that this was where the aunt had hidden the keys, but knew her husband would dismiss this idea as nonsense. So over breakfast she casually suggested that when they searched the house again they should run their fingers along the door lintels 'just in case'. He went off saying they would, but why on earth would she put her car keys on top of a door, when her handbag was the most obvious place to keep them alongside everything else?

Later that morning he phoned to say that he had found the keys behind a loose piece of wallpaper on the lintel above the kitchen door. She asked him to describe where they were and he said the wallpaper was loose towards the right-hand end. He also said that the wallpaper was a flowered design which matched her dream. When he returned home feeling very triumphant, she told him about her dream, which he dismissed as chance coincidence occasioned by them talking about it. Later, thinking it over, they decided that she probably put them up there in case of being burgled by anyone intent on stealing her car, who would obviously search her handbag. She had been a tall woman so it was easy for her to do.

Dowsing for pipes

One morning in late September 2017, I gave the same talk to members of a Probus club. For those who have not heard of 'Probus' it is an international organisation for retired professional and business people. Probus was originally for men only, as that club still was at the time of my talk, but now includes women. My post coffee audience comprised some 60 elderly men who, to my surprise as I expected much scepticism, took a keen interest in the subject. Anyway, during post talk discussion, the subject somehow turned

Discussion

from telepathy to dowsing. Many of the audience had been involved in post WW2 construction of large-scale water, gas and oil facilities across the world, including the Middle East in desert areas. One after another, they said that when working in the desert far away from towns, their workforce always included a dowser for successful location of water or whatever they were looking for, and gave many examples of apparently successful dowsing. I must stress that those who spoke about their experiences, many ex-WW2 military men, were talking in a straightforward 'This is what happened, I was there and I saw it' way.

One Probus member then told us the following story. During the 1990s his firm was contracted to help build a new factory in Essex. Between the road and the site was a wide patch of boggy ground under which there were said to be old water pipes, but they did not know where they were. As the site manager, he phoned the local water board for help, and a young man in a small van duly arrived. After they had shown him the area he went back to the van, and they expected him to return with some sophisticated ground radar detection device. To their astonishment he came back with two wire dowsing rods and proceeded to crisscross the ground, marking with stones the point where the rods turned inwards to give the lie of the pipes. After he left, and in a state of disbelief, they very cautiously dug down to check, and there the pipes were, so they were able to negotiate a crossing with safety. But there is a personal end note to this story, which is what lifts it out of the ordinary.

On his return home he was so fascinated by what had happened that he felt that he had to try dowsing for himself, so he fashioned a couple of rods from wire coat hangers. If he had the skill it would be invaluable at work. To his surprise the dowsing rods crossed at points as he crisscrossed his garden hoping to track the course of a water pipe. When he dug down he found that he had dowsed correctly. He then managed to do the same for a neighbour who wanted to sink foundations for a large patio, and then for a neighbour who wanted to plant some trees. Some months later he was asked by another neighbour to trace a pipe, but feeling very foolish and embarrassed, he failed completely. The rods just swung aimlessly, and to his baffled disappointment the ability has never returned. When I asked him what he had felt during the successful dowsing occasions when the rods crossed over each other, he said that he seemed to be in what he could only describe as an oddly detached state of mind in which he somehow "just knew". He didn't quite know what he meant by this, but has never been able to enter this odd state of mind again.

Dowsing for pipes with 'Old Bert'

While still on the subject of dowsing, here is my only family story of anything ESP. My father (born, 1905) was a tough countryman, brought up on a large country estate in Surrey where his father was the gamekeeper. He had little time for religion, even less for politics – especially the local council – and believed only what he could see and touch. Despite his general scepticism concerning anything psi, he had one experience that he was unable to explain. As a young man in the 1920s he was one of a gang sent to drain a boggy area of the estate. With no ground plans no one knew where the old pipes were, so, after some desultory digging round, they gave up and waited for 'Old Bert' the foreman. After looking at the area 'Old Bert' cut a 'Y' shaped hazel wand, put stones in his pockets, held the wand straight out in front of him with the arms slightly stretched apart to give it some spring, and steadily crisscrossed across the ground. Each time the wand dipped down he placed a stone. The young lads jeered in disbelief, saying that he knew where the pipes were all along. My father volunteered to have a go, but nothing happened when he held the wand so he was asked to try again – but this time with 'Old Bert' right behind him with his hands holding my father's wrists. This time, when they crossed an unseen pipe, my father felt the wand twist down strongly in his hands, but when 'Old Bert' let go, nothing happened. When they dug down, there were the old, broken, pipes.

The bee sting

My next-door neighbour was manager of our local social services. One day, chairing a meeting concerning new policy initiatives, she felt an overpowering urge to go back to her office. Feeling baffled, as she could think of no reason, she made her excuses and hurried back. On arrival her secretary told her that her daughter's school wanted her to telephone them as soon as possible. When she phoned the school they said that her six-year-old daughter had been stung on her inner thigh by a bee, that it was red, swollen and very painful and she was crying for mum to come and collect her. Her daughter loved school, so she had no reason to feel worried about her. But it seems that in her distress her daughter was telepathically calling for her that afternoon.

My own position regarding psi

It would be natural for any reader to believe that I must have some emotional stake in promoting belief in psi through personal experiences. But, frustratingly, I have never knowingly had an ESP or PK experience in my life. If there are genes that code for psi, and I think that there must be, then mine are deeply recessive. In this book I have tried to present the empirical evidence for some forms of psychokinetic effect when people are in the psi frame of mind and the facts are fully referenced. My interpretations, based on my 'two state of mind' hypothesis, are open to dispute, but that does not invalidate the evidence on which the hypothesis is based.

Closing comments

I hope that sceptics of psi healing will study the empirical findings and, if they are unable to disprove them, admit that the evidence for psi healing is strong. The same goes for the other psi phenomena. Whether my 'two states of mind' hypothesis will be supported by further investigation remains to be seen. It seems to fit with the mental circumstances in which ESP and PK phenomena occur, and is in agreement with how people describe their state of mind during a psi experience. If, in the light of all the empirical and verified anecdotal evidence now available, psi is accepted as a genuine phenomenon, a new theory of mind must inevitably emerge that will include how the mental world of our experiencing and the inferred physical world of the sciences, which includes our brain, interact.

APPENDIX A

Society for Psychical Research Presidents

Physicists, Astronomers, Mathematicians

1885-1887
Balfour Stewart (1827-1887): Physicist, Professor of Physics at Queen's College, Manchester, from 1870, Fellow of the Royal Society from 1862.

1896-1899
Sir William Crookes (1832-1919): Chemist and physicist, discoverer of thallium and cathode rays, inventor of radiometer.

1901-1903 (and 1932)
Sir Oliver Lodge (1851-1940): Physicist and mathematician, Professor of Physics and Mathematics, University of Liverpool from 1881 First Principal of University of Birmingham.

1904- 1905
Sir William Fletcher Barrett (1845-1925): Physicist; Chair of Physics, Royal College of Science, Dublin, Fellow of the Royal Society from 1899.

1908-1909 (and 1932)
Eleanor Sidgwick (1845-1936): Mathematician. Principal of Newnham College, Cambridge (first women's college), 1892-1910.

1919-
John William Strutt, 3rd Baron Rayleigh (1842-1919): Experimental physicist, Fellow of Trinity College, Cambridge, from 1866.
Nobel Prize for Physics, 1904

1923
Camille Flammarion (1842-1925): French astronomer, President of the Astronomical Society of France.

1937-1938
Robert John Strutt, 4th Baron Rayleigh (1875-1947): Physicist; Professor of Physics, Imperial College, London, 1908-1919, Fellow of the Royal Society from 1905.

1945-1946
George N.M. Tyrrell (1879-1952): Mathematician and physicist; worked with Marconi on radio communications.

1950-1951
Samuel George Soal (1890-1975). Mathematician. Senior lecturer in mathematics, Queen Mary College, London.

Society for Psychical Research Presidents

1953-1955
F.J.M. Stratton (1881-1961): Astrophysicist, Professor of Astrophysics and Director of Solar Physics Observatory at University of Cambridge 1928-1947, President of Gonville and Caius College, Cambridge 1945-1948.

1976-1979 (and 1981-1982)
Arthur J. Ellison (1920-2000): Technologist; Senior lecturer, Queen Mary College, London from 1972 then Head of the Department of Electrical and Electronic Engineering, City University, London.

1993-1995
Archie Roy: Astronomer; Professor Emeritus of Astronomy, University of Glasgow, founder of the Scottish SPR in 1987.

2000-2004
Bernard Carr: Professor in Mathematics and Astronomy, Queen Mary & Westfield College, London.

Physiologists, Biologists, Doctors, Zoologists, Anthropologists

1905
Charles Richet (1850-1935): French physiologist, Professor of Physiology at the Faculty of Medicine of Paris, (Nobel Prize winner 1913).

1911
Andrew Lang (1844-1912). Anthropologist. Fellow of Merton College, Cambridge.

1922
Thomas Walter Mitchell (1869-1944). Physician. Editor of the *British Journal of Medical Psychology*.

1926-1927
Hans Driesch (1867-1941). German biologist and natural philosopher; Professor of Systematic Philosophy at Cologne University from 1919, Director of Philosophical Seminars at Leipzig from 1921.

1965-1969
Sir Alister Hardy (1896-1985). Professor of Zoology, Hull University. Linacre Professor of Zoology, Oxford University. Founder of the Religious Experience Research Unit, Manchester College, Oxford.

1969-1971
William A. H. Rushton (1901-1980). Physiologist, Professor of Physiology, Trinity College, Cambridge.

2005-2007 (2015-2018)
John Poynton: Emeritus Professor of Biology, University of Natal; Scientific Fellow of the Zoological Society of London; Associate of the Natural History Museum, London.

APPENDIX B

Society for Psychical Research Presidents

Philosophers, Classicists, Psychologists

1882-1884 and 1888-1892
Henry Sidgwick (1838-1900): Philosopher. Knightsbridge Professor of Moral Philosophy, University of Cambridge.

1893
Arthur Balfour (1848-1930): Philosopher. Trinity College, Cambridge. Prime Minister 1902-1905.

1894-1895
William James (1842-1910): Psychologist and philosopher. Chair of Psychology and Emeritus Professor of Philosophy, Harvard University.

1900
Frederic William Henry Myers (1843-1901): Classical scholar and philosopher, Fellow, Trinity College, Cambridge.

1906-1907
Gerald Balfour (1854-1945): Classics Tripos, 1st class Honours., Trinity College, Cambridge. Fellow, Trinity College. Honorary LLD, University of Cambridge. Member, Privy Council.

1913-1914
Henri Bergson (1859-1941): Philosopher. Chair of the Philosophy of History at the College de France 1900-1921. Nobel Prize for Literature, 1927.

1914-15
Ferdinand Canning Scott Schiller (1864-1937): Philosopher; Professor of Philosophy at the University of South California from 1929.

1915-1916 and 1952
Gilbert Murray (1866-1957): Classical scholar, Fellow of New College, Oxford, later Regius Professor of Greek. Founded the League of Nations Union after World War I.

1917-1918
Laurence Pearsall Jacks (1860-1955): Philosopher. Professor of Philosophy, Manchester College, Oxford from 1903, College Principal from 1951. Editor of Hibbert Journal.

1935-1936 and 1958-1960
Charlie Dunbar Broad (1887-1971): Philosopher. Knightsbridge Professor of Moral Philosophy, University of Cambridge. Received Fellowships and honorary degrees from several countries.

Society for Psychical Research

1939-1941
Henry Habberley Price (1899-1984): Philosopher. Wykeham Professor of Logic, Faculty of Philosophy, University of Oxford.

1942-1944
Robert Henry Thouless (1894-1984) Psychologist. Reader in Educational Psychology. Cambridge.

1947-1948
William Henry Salter (1880-1969): Classical scholar, Trinity College, Cambridge and Barrister-at-Law. Called to the Bar 1905.

1949-1950
Gardner Murphy (1895-1979). Psychologist. Hodgson Fellow, Harvard University. Professor of Psychology, Menninger Foundation. Visiting Professor of Psychology, George Washington University.

1960-1963
Eric Robertson Dodds (1893-1979). Classical scholar. Regius Professor of Greek, Oxford.

1971-1974
Clement William Kennedy Mundle (1920-1989): Philosopher. Head of Philosophy Departments first at University of Dundee, then at University College, North Wales.

1974-1976
John Beloff (1920 -2006). Senior Lecturer in Psychology, University of Edinburgh and instrumental in establishing the Koestler Chair at Edinburgh.

1980
Joseph Banks Rhine (1895-1980). Botanist, psychologist, and parapsychologist. Founder of the Parapsychology Laboratory, Duke University, USA.

1980
Louise Ella Rhine (1891-1983). Botanist, psychologist and parapsychologist. Co-worker with her husband, J.B. Rhine.

1984-1988
Donald, J. West. Psychologist and Criminologist. Director of the Institute of Criminology, Cambridge. Fellow of Darwin College, Cambridge. Several times Vice President,

1988-1989
Ian Stevenson. Psychiatrist. Director of Division of Personality Studies, Carlson Professor of Psychiatry, University of Virginia. Researcher into claims of reincarnation.

1989-1992
Alan Gauld. Psychologist. Retired Reader in Psychology, University of Nottingham.

1995-1998
David Fontana. Psychologist. Professor of Educational Psychology, Universities of Minho and Algarve. Distinguished Visiting Fellow, University of Wales, Cardiff.

2007-2011
Deborah Delanoy. Psychologist. Professor of Psychology, University of Northampton. Research Director, School of Behavioural Studies, Director, Centre for the Study of Anomalous Psychological Processes, Northampton.

2011-2015
Richard Broughton. Psychologist. Former Director, Rhine Research Centre. Durham, USA. Researcher into anomalous intuition, Centre for the Study of Anomalous Psychological Processes. University of Northampton.

2018-2021
Chris Roe, Psychologist. Professor of Psychology, University of Northampton. Director, Centre for the Study of Anomalous Psychological Processes. Northampton.

2021-
Adrian Parker. Psychologist. Professor of Psychology, Gothenberg University, Sweden.

References

1

Bengston, W. (2010) *The Energy Cure: Unravelling the mystery of Hands-On Healing.* Toronto, Key Porter Books.

Bengston, W. F (2010) Breakthrough: Clues to healing with intention. *Edge Science* No2: 5-9. pdf. www.scientificexploration.org/edgescience

Bengston, W. (2017) Some Reflections on Consciousness, Intention, and Healing. In *Being & Biology: Is Consciousness the Life Force?* Dunne, B,. Jahn, R. (eds)

Bengston, W. F. (2019) Examining Biological and Physical Correlates to Anomalous Healing. *Journal of the American Holistic Veterinary Medical Association.* 55, 14-25

Bengston, W., Krinsley, D. (2000) The effect of the 'laying on of hands' on transplanted breast cancer in mice. *Journal Scientific Exploration.* 14(3): 353-364

Bengston, W., Moga, M. (2007) Resonance, Placebo Effects and Type 11 Errors: Some implications from healing research for experimental methods. *Journal Alternative & Complementary Medicine 13*(3): 317-327

Benor, D. J. (2001). *Spiritual Healing: Scientific Validation of a Healing Revolution.* USA: Vision Publishing.

Broderick, D., Goertzel, B. (2015) *Evidence for Psi: Thirteen Empirical Research Reports.* Eds. Jefferson Nc. McFarland & Co.

Bunnell, T. (1996) The effect of hands-on healing on enzyme activity. *International Journal of Research in Complementary Medicine.* 3, 265-340.

Bunnell, T. (1999) The effect of 'Healing with intent' on pepsin enzyme activity. *Journal of Scientific Exploration.* 3(2) 139-148.

Buxton-King, A. (2004) *The NHS Healer: How my son's life inspired a healing journey.* London, Virgin Books.

Buxton-King. A. (2017) *The NHS Healer: Onwards and Upwards.* Cambridge, UK. Vanguard Press.

Coates, M. (2001). Healing for Horses. London, Rider.

Coates, M. (2003) Hands-On Healing for Pets: The Animal Lover's Essential Guide to Using Healing Energy. London, Rider.

Cohen, J. (1997) Doctors told me I had only eight months to live. Interview. *Daily Mail.* 2nd October, p.48.

de Melo M. P. B. X., Rodrigues C. D. S., Dos Santos D. A., de Melo J. K. X., Tokeshi H. (2021). Alternative treatment with Johrei: a controlled randomized study evaluating seed physiological potential. New York. Explore 17 (1) 32-39. https://doi.org/10.1016/j.explore.2020.07.012

References

De Souza, A. L. T., Rosa, D. P. C., Blanco, B. A., Passaglia, P., Stabile, A. M. (2017). Effects of therapeutic touch on healing of skin in rats. *Explore 13*,5,333-338. Doi: 10.1016/j.explore.2017.06.006

Edwards, S. (2017) *Healing in a Hospital: Scientific Evidence that Spiritual Healing improves Health.* CreateSpace. Self-published.

Goffaux, P., Redmond, W. J., Rainville, P., Marchand, S. (2007 Descending analgesia – when the spine echoes what the brain expects. *Pain. 130*, 1-2.

Grad, B., Cadoret, R., Paul, G. I. (1961) An unorthodox treatment of wound healing in mice. *International Journal of Parapsychology. 3* (1) 5-24.

Grad, B. (1963) A telekinetic effect on plant growth I. *International Journal of Parapsychology. 5* 2) 117-134.

Grad, B. (1964) A telekinetic effect on plant growth II. Experiments involving treatment of saline in stoppered bottles. *International Journal of Parapsychology. 6* (4), 473-478

Grad, B. (1965) Some biological effects of laying-on of hands: a review of experiments with animals and plants. *Journal American Society for Psychical Research. 59*, 95-127. Reproduced in Schmeidler, Gertrude (ed) in *Parapsychology: its relation to physics, biology, psychology and psychiatry.* Metuchen, NJ. Scarecrow Books. 1976.

Gronowicz, G. A., Jhaveri, A. & Clarke, L. W., Aronow. M. S., Smith, T. H. (2008). Therapeutic touch stimulates the proliferation of human cells in culture. *Journal of Alternative and Complementary Medicine. 14* (3) 233-239.

Jain, S. (2021) *Healing Ourselves: Biofield Science and the Future of Health.* Boulder.
Sounds True Publishers.

Jonas, W. B.. Crawford, C. C. (2003). *Healing, Intention and Energy Medicine: Science, Research Methods and Clinical Implications*. Edinburgh: Churchill Livingstone.

Lee, R. T., Kinstone, T., Roberts, L., Edwards, S., Soundy, A., Shah, P. R., Haque, M. S., Singh, S. (2017) A pragmatic randomised controlled trial of healing therapy in a gastroenterology outpatient setting. *European Journal of Integrative Medicine.* 9, 110-119.

Manning, M. (1996) *No Faith Required*. Oslo. Eikstein Publ.

Moga, M. M. (2017) Exceptional experiences of healers: A survey of Healing Touch practitioners and students. *Journal of Exceptional Experiences and Psychology.* 5, 1, 24-34.

Monzillo, E., Gronowicz, G. A. (2011) New insights on therapeutic touch: A discussion of experimental methodology and design that resulted in significant effects on normal human cells and osteosarcoma. *Explore,* 7, (1) 44-51. doi:10.1016/j.explore.2010.10.001.

Murray D., Stoessl A. J. (2013). Mechanisms and therapeutic implications of the placebo effect in neurological and psychiatric conditions. *Pharmacology & Therapeutics 140 (3):* 30618. doi:10.1016/j.pharmthera.2013.07.009.

Nash, C. (1982) Psychokinetic control of bacterial growth. *Journal of the Society for Psychical Research.* 51, 217-221

Rahtz, E., Child, S., Knight, S., Warber, S. L., Dieppe, P. (2019) Clients of UK healers: A mixed methods survey of their demography, health problems, and experiences of healing. *Complementary Therapies in Clinical Practice.* 35, 72-77

Rein, G. (1978) *Healing energy and neurochemistry*. Paper, 2nd International Conference of the Society for Psychical Research, Cambridge, UK.

Roe, C. A., Sonnex, C., Roxburgh, E. C. (2015) Two meta-analyses of noncontact healing studies. *Explore.11*,1,11-20. http://dx.doi.org/10.1016/j.explore.2014.10.001

Smith, M. J. (1968) Paranormal effects on enzyme activity. Abstract. *Journal of Parapsychology. 32*, 281

Smith, M. J. (1972) The influence on enzyme growth by the "laying on of hands". *The Dimensions of Healing: A Symposium.* Los Altos, CA. The Academy of Parapsychology and Medicine.

Soundy, A., Lee, R., Kingstone, T., Singh, H., Shah, P. P., Edwards, S., Roberts, L. (2015). Experiences with healing therapy in patients with irritable bowel syndrome and inflammatory bowel disease. *BioMed Central.*

Trivedi, M. K., Pait, I. S., Shettigar, H., Gangwar, M., Jana, S. (2015) In vitro evaluation of biofield treatment on cancer biomarkers involved in endometrial and prostate cancer cell lines. *Cancer, 7 (8)* 253-257. Doi: 10.4172/1948-5956.1000358

Vernon, D. (2021) *Dark Cognition: Evidence for Psi and its implications for Consciousness.* London. Routledge.

Yount, G. L., Patil, S., Dave, U., Alves-dos-Santos, L., Gon, K., Arauz, R., Rachlin, K. (2012). Evaluation of biofield treatment dose and distance in a model of cancer cell death. *Journal of Alternative and Complementary Medicine. 19*,(2) 124-127

2

Achterberg, J., Cooke, K., Richards, T., Standish, L. J., Kozak, L., Lake, J. (2005). Evidence for correlations between distant intentionality and brain function in recipients: a functional magnetic imaging analysis. *Journal of Alternative and Complementary Medicine* 11 (6): 965-971

Bengston, W. F., Krinsley, D. (2000) The effect of 'laying on of hands' on transplanted breast cancer in mice. *Journal of Scientific Exploration* 14 (3): 353-364

Bengston, W. F., Moga, M. (2007) Resonance, Placebo Effects and Type II Errors: Some implications from Healing Research for Experimental Methods. *Journal of Alternative and Complementary Medicine* 13 (3): 317-327.

Benor, D. J. (2002) *Spiritual Healing: Scientific Validation of a Healing Revolution.* Healing. Research Volume 1. Professional Supplement. Southfield, MI/Vision Publications.

Cade, Maxwell, C., Coxhead, N. (1979) *the Awakened Mind: Biofeedback and the Development of Higher States of Awareness.* Shaftesbury, Element Books.

Charman, R. (2006a) Has direct brain to brain communication been demonstrated by electroencephalographic monitoring of paired or group subjects? *JSPR* , 70, 1-24

Charman, R. (2006b) Direct brain to brain communication – further evidence from EEG and fMRI studies. *Para Rev, 40.* 3-9

Charman, R. (2006c) Something really is going on. *JSPR.* Vol 70: 249-51

Hendricks, L., Bengston W. F., Gunkelman, J. (2010) the Healing Connection: EEG Harmonics, Entrainment, and Schumann's Resonances. *Journal of Scientific Exploration.* 24(4):655-666

Jonas, W.B., Crawford, C. C., eds. (2003) *Healing Intention: Science, research methods and clinical implications.* Edinburgh. Churchill Livingstone.

Lazslo, E. (2003) *The Connectivity Hypothesis.* Albany, New York Press.

Macmanaway, B., Turcan, T. (1983) *Healing: The Energy that can Restore Health.* Wellingborough, Thorsons Publishers.

Sagi, M. (2021) *Remote Healing: Nonlocal Information Medicine and the Akashic Field.* Foreword by Ervin Laszlo. Rochester, Vermont. Healing Arts Press.

Wise, A. (2004) *The High Performance Mind: Mastering brainwaves for insight, healing and creativity.* New York, Tarcher/Putnam. 2nd ed.

www.mindmirroreeg.com/w MaxwellCade.htm. The Life and Work of C. Maxwell Cade – Mind Mirror EEG.

3

Aron, E., Aron, A. (1981). *Experimental interventions of high coherence groups into disorderly social systems,* Paper presented at the American Psychological Association Annual Conference, Los Angeles.

Aron, E., Aron, A. (1986). *The Maharishi Effect: A Revolution Through Meditation.* Walpole, NH. Stillpoint.

Benor, D. J. (2002) *Spiritual Healing: Scientific Validation of a Healing Revolution.* Southfield, MI. Vision Publications.

Borland, C., Landrith, G. (1974). Improved quality of city life through the Transcendental Meditation program: Decreased crime rate. Fairfield, Iowa. *Scientific Research* on the *Transcendental Meditation and TM-Sidhi Program: Collected Papers*, 1978. Orme-Johnson, D. W., Farrow, J. T. (eds) MIU Press.

Cade, M. C., Coxhead N. (1979). *The Awakened Mind*. Shaftesbury, UK. Element Books.

Charman, R. A. (2021) Empirical evidence that psi healing in mice confirms parapsychology, or psiology as a legitimate scientific discipline. *Journal of the Society for Psychical Research*, 85, 91-103

Davies, J. L., Alexander C. N. (1979). The Maharishi Technology of the Unified Field and Improved Quality of life in the United States: A study of the First World Peace Assembly, Amherst, Massachusetts. *Scientific Research on Transcendental Meditation and TM-Sidhi. Program: Collected Papers*. Vol 4.1986. Chalmers, R. A., Clements, G., Schenkluhn H., Weinless, M. (eds) MIU Press.

Deshpande, P., Kowall, J. P. (2017). Explanation of the Maharishi Effect by Holographic Principle. *Journal of Consciousness Exploration and Research*. 8 (10), 797-805.

Dillbeck, M. C., Foss, A., Zimmerman, W. J., (1984). Maharishi's Global Ideal Society Campaign Improved quality of life in Rhode Island through The Transcendental Meditation and TM-Sidhi program. Fairfield, Iowa. *Scientific Research on the Transcendental Meditation and TM-Sidhi Program: Collected Papers*, Vol 4. 1986, Chalmers, R. A., Clements, G., Schenkluhn, H., Weinless, M. (eds) MIU Press.

Dillbeck, M. C., Landrith, G., Orme-Johnson, D. W. (1981). The Transcendental Meditation programme and crime rate change in a sample of 48 cities. *Journal of Crime and Justice* 4, 24-25.

References

Goyal, M., Singh, S., Sibinga, E. M., Gould, N. F., Rowland-Seymour, A., Sharma,

R., Berger, Z., Sleicher, D., Maron, D. D., Shihab, M., Ranasinghe, P. D., Linn, S., Saha, S., Bass, E. B., Haythornthwaite, J. A. (2014). Meditation programs for psychological stress and wellbeing: Systematic review and meta-analysis. *Journal of the American Medical Association, Internal Medicine.* 174, 3:357- 368 (March).

Hagelin, J. S. (1987). Is Consciousness the Unified Field? A Field Theorist's Perspective. *Modern Science and Vedic Science*, 1, 29–87.

Jonas, W. B., Crawford, C. C. (2003) *Healing, Intention and Energy Medicine: Science, Research Methods and Clinical Indications.* Edinburgh, Churchill Livingstone.

Laszlo, E. (1996). *The Whispering Pond.* Rockport, MA. Element Books.

Maharishi Effect. Free download papers. https://anantidotetoviolence.org/.../research-*on-the-maharishi-effect*

Montecucco, N. (2000). *Cyber: La Visione Olistica.* Rome.

Orme-Johnson, D. W. Truth About TM. http://www.truthabouttm.org/truth/SocietalEffects/Rationale-Research/index.cfm

Orme-Johnson, D. W., Oates, R. M (2009). A Field-Theoretic View of Consciousness: Reply to Critics. *Journal of Scientific Exploration.* Vol 23, 2: 139-166

Orme-Johnson, D., Dillbeck, M. C., Wallace, R. K., Landreth G. S. (1982). Intersubject EEG Coherence: Is Consciousness a Field? *International Journal of Neuroscience.* Vol 16, 203-209.

Roe, C. A., Sonnex, C., Roxburgh, E. C. (2015). Two meta-analyses of noncontact healing studies. *Explore.* 11, 1,11-23. http://dx.doi.org/10.1016/j.explore.2014.10.001

Schrodt, P. A. (1990). "A methodological critique of a test of the Maharishi

technology of the unified field". Journal of Conflict Resolution. 34 (4): 745– 755.

Shearer, A. (1982). *Effortless Being: The Yoga Sutras of Patanjali.* London, Wildwood House Ltd.

Wallace, R. K. (1986). *The Neurophysiology of Enlightenment.* Fairfield. Iowa. Dharma Publications.

Wallace, R. K. (1993) *The Physiology of Consciousness.* Fairfield, Iowa. MIU Press.

Zimmerman, J. (1979). Improved quality of life during the Rhode Island Ideal Society Campaign, Phase 1, June 12 to September 12, 1978. Unpublished Report available from MIU, 1A 52556.

4

Bellg, L. (2016) *Near Death in the ICU: Stories from patients near death and why we should listen to them.* Appleton. Wiscon. Sloan Press.

Borjigin, J., *et al.* (2013). Surge of neurophysiological coherence and connectivity in the dying brain. *Proceedings of the National Academy of Science,* 110 (35), 14432-14437. Available at http://www.pnas.org/content/110/35/14432.full.pdf

Borjigin, J., Wang, M. M., & Mashour, G. A. (2013). Reply to Greyson: Experimental evidence lays the foundation for a rational understanding of near-death experiences. *Proceedings of the National Academy of Science, 110*(47): E4406 Published online 2013 Nov 6.doi: 10.1073/pnas.131758110

Chawla, L. S., Akst, S., Junker, C., Jacobs, B., & Seneff, M. G. (2009). Surges of electroencephalogram activity at the time of death: A case series. *Journal of Palliative Medicine, 12,* 1095-1100.

Fenwick, P. & Fenwick, E. (1995) *The Truth in the Light: An investigation of over 300 near-death experiences.* London, Headline Book Publishing.

Greyson, B., Kelly, E. F. & Dunseath, W. J. R. (2013). Surge of neurophysiological activity in the dying brain. *Proceedings of the National Academy of Science,* 110(47): E4405. Published online 2013 November 6. doi: 10.1073/pnas.1316937110 PMCID: PMC3839773 Neuroscience.

Lommel van, P. (2010). *Consciousness beyond life: The science of near-death experience.* New York: Harper One.

Moody, R. (1975). *Life after life.* New York: Bantam Books.

Parnia, S. (2005). *What happens when we die? A groundbreaking study into the nature of life and death.* London: Hay House.

Parnia, S. (2013). *Erasing death: The science that is rewriting the boundaries between life and death.* New York: HarperCollins.

Rivas, T., Dirwen, A., Smit, H., & May, R. (2016). *The self does not die: Verified paranormal phenomena from near-death experiences.* International Association for Near-Death Studies.

Rommer, B. R. (2000) *Blessing in Disguise: Another side of the near-death experience.* St. Paul, MN. Llewellyn.

Sartori, P. (2008). *The near-death experiences of hospitalized intensive care patients: A five-year clinical study.* New York: Edwin Mellen Press.

Sartori, P. (2014). *The wisdom of near-death experiences: How understanding NDEs can help us live more fully.* London: Watkins Publications.

5

Barrington, M. R. (1991). JOTT – Just One of Those Things. *Psi Researcher 3*, 5-6.

Barrington, M. R. (2018*) JOTT: When things disappear ... come back and relocate – and why it really happens* (2018)

Jinks, T. (2018) *Disappearing Object Phenomenon – An Investigation.* Jefferson, NC McFarland & Co.

6

Batcheldor, K. J. (1965-66). Report on a case of table levitation and associated phenomena. *Journal of the Society for Psychical Research* 43:339-56.

Batcheldor, K. (1984). Contributions to the theory of PK induction from sitter-group work. *Journal of the American Society for Psychical Research* 78:105-22.

Batcheldor, K. & Giesler, P. 1994). Notes on the elusiveness problem in relation to a radical view of paranormality. *Journal of the American Society for Psychical Research* 88: 91-111

Brookes-Smith, C. (1973) Data-tape recorded experimental PK phenomena. *Journal of the Society for Psychical Research* 47: 69-89.

Brookes-Smith, C. & Hunt, D. W. (1970) Some experiments in psychokinesis. *Journal of the Society for Psychical Research* 45: 265-81.

Owen A. R. G. (1964) *Can We Explain the Poltergeist?* Taplinger Publ. Co. New York.

Owen, I. M. & Sparrow, M. (1976) *Conjuring up Philip. An Adventure in Psychokinesis.* Harper & Row. New York.

Randall, J. (1082) *Psychokinesis: A Study of Paranormal Forces Through The Ages.* London. Souvenir Press.

Rovelli, C. (2016) *Seven Brief Lessons in Physics.* London. Penguin Books.

Rovelli, C. (2017) *Reality Is Not What It Seems: The Journey to Quantum Gravity.* London. Penguin Books.

7

Colvin, B. G. (2008) The Andover Case: A responsive rapping poltergeist. *JSPR* 72, 1-20

Colvin, B. G. (2010) The acoustic properties of unexplained rapping sounds. *JSPR* 74, 65-93

Gauld, A., Cornell, A. D. (1979). *Poltergeists.* London, Routledge & Kegan Paul.

8

Carpenter, J. C. (2012) *First Sight: ESP and parapsychology in everyday life.* Rowman & Littlefield, Lanham, Maryland, USA.

Carter, C. (2007). *Parapsychology and the Skeptics: A scientific argument for the existence of ESP.* Pittsburgh: PAJA Books.

Freeman, D. (2004) One in a million. *New York Review of Books, 51,* p. 5. (Review of *Debunked, ESP, Telekinesis, and other Pseudoscience* by Georges Charpak and Henri Broch. Translated from the French title of *Devenez, Sorciers, Devenez Savants.*)

Gauld, A. & Cornell, A. D. (1979). *Poltergeists.* London: Routledge & Kegan Paul.

Haynes, R. (1961) *The Hidden Springs: An Inquiry into Extra-Sensory Perception.* London, Hutchinson.

Haynes, R. (1976). *The Seeing Eye, The Seeing I: Perception, Sensory and Extra-Sensory.* New York. St Martin's Press.

Jahn, R., Dunne, B. J. (1987) *Margins of Reality: The role of consciousness in the physical world.* Harcourt Brace, New York.

Jonas, W. A., Crawford, C. C. (2003) *Healing, Intention & Energy Medicine: Science Research Methods and Clinical Implications.* Churchill Livingstone, New York.

Kuhn, T. S. (1962). *The Structure of Scientific Revolutions.* Chicago. University of Chicago Press.

Le Shan, L. (1980) *Clairvoyant Reality: Towards a general theory of the paranormal.* Turnstone Press, Wellingborough, UK.

REFERENCES

Le Shan, L. (2009) *A New Science of the Paranormal.* Quest Books, Wheaton, Illinois.

Mangulus, Deb. (http://debmangulus.wordpress.com)

Mayer, E. L. (1996) 'Subjectivity and intersubjectivity of clinical facts,' *International Journal of Psychoanalysis* 77:709-737

Mayer, E. L. (2001) "On Telepathic Dreams?": An Unpublished Paper by Robert Stoller. *Journal of the American Psychoanalytic Association.* 49 (2): 638.

Mayer, E. L. (2007) *Extraordinary Knowing: Science, scepticism, and the inexplicable powers of the human mind.* Forewords by Freeman Dyson, physicist and mathematician, and Carol Gilligan, Professor, social psychology, New York University. Bantam Books, New York.

McMoneagle, J. (1993) *Mind Trek: Exploring Consciousness, Time and Space through Remote Viewing.* Charlottesville, VA. Hampton Roads.

Mossbridge, J., Tressoldi P. and Utts J. (2012) Predictive physiological anticipation preceding seemingly unpredictable stimuli: a meta-analysis. Front. Psychology 3:390. doi: 10.3389/fpsyg.2012.00390

Newberg, A., D'Aquili, E., Rause, V. (2001) *Why God won't go away: Brain Science and the Biology of Belief.* Ballantine Books, New York.

Palmer, Helen. (www.enneagram.com)

Parker. A. (2003) "We ask does psi exist? But is it the right question?" *Journal of Consciousness Studies.* 19 (7): 128

Radin, D. (2006). *Entangled minds: Extrasensory experiences in a quantum reality.* New York: Paraview Pocket Books.

Schiltz, M. J., Honorton, C. (1992) (1985 reprint). Ganzfeld Psi performance within an artistically gifted population. *Journal of the American Society for Psychical Research.* 86: 83-88.

Tadd, Ellen. (www.ellentadd.com also www.montaguepress.com)

Tart, C. T., Puthoff, H. E., Targ, R. (2002) *Mind at Large: IEEE Symposium on the Nature of Extrasensory Perception.* Charlottesville, VA. Hampton Roads.

Ullman, M., Krippner, S., Vaughan, A. (1973) *Dream Telepathy: Experiments in Nocturnal Perception,* Hampton Roads, Charlottesville, VA (Reissued 2002, 3rd edn. Studies in Consciousness series with new Introductions).

Wilkins, H., Sherman, H. M. (2004). *Thoughts through space.* Charlottesville, VA: Hampton Roads.

Williams, B. J. (2015) *Psychic Phenomena and the Brain: Exploring the Neurophysiology of Psi.* Australian Institute of Parapsychological Research Inc. Gladesville, NSW. Monograph No.3.

Worrall, A. A., Worrall, O. N. (1965) *The Gift of Healing.* Ariel Press, Winchester, Ohio.

9

Edwards, S. (2021) *Spiritual Healing in Hospitals and Clinics: Scientific Evidence that Energy Medicine promotes speedy recovery and positive outcomes.* Rochester, Vermont. Findhorn Press.

Feather, S. R., Schmicker, M. (2005) *The Gift: the Extraordinary Paranormal Experiences of Ordinary People.* London. Rider.

REFERENCES

Mayer, E. L. (2007) *Extraordinary Knowing: Science, Skepticism, and the inexplicable powers of the human Mind.* New York, Bantam Books.

Notes

1. https://www.bengstonresearch.com/publications
2. Revised and developed from 'Maxwell Cade's Mind Mirror: A call for renewed research into claimed healer/healee EEG profile correlation during a healing session using new generation EEG applications.' PR Issue 70: 14-22. (April, 2014).
3. See also more recent peer reviewed papers on the Maharishi Effect. (https://anantidotetoviolence.org/.../research-on-the-maharishi-effect).Incomplete link?
4. Revised and developed from 'Mainstream sociological theory does not include the claim that Group Meditation can influence surrounding societal behaviour – but does recent Psi research support this claim as possible in principle, so possible in practice? JSPR 86 (1)
5. This is the YouTube link for the 11-minute video: https://www.youtube.com/watch?v=X2lGPT2J1cc

    This is the YouTube link for the 41-minute video: https://www.youtube.com/watch?v=tSFkxkrSM90

    Revised and developed from 'Conjuring up "Philip"'. PR. 48:16-22 (2008)
6. Developed from correspondence: JR. 74:286-287 (2010), and JR. 75: 61-63 (2011)

[7] Revised into single chapter format from:

'Some reflections on the loss and return of a small harp' *PR.* 61: 28-31 (2012)

'After Dr Mayer said, "*This changes everything*" What happened next? Part One.' *PR.* 62: 27-32 (2012).

'After Dr Mayer said, "*This changes everything*" What happened next? Part Two.' *PR.* 63:27-30 (2012)

'After Dr Mayer said, "*This changes everything*" What happened next? Part Three.' *PR.*64:22-25 (2012)

'After Dr Mayer said "*This changes everything*" What happened next? Part Four. *PR* 65: 13-18 (2013)

About the Author

Robert Charman is a member of the Society for Psychical Research and Scientific and Medical Network. He has published over 40 papers on ESP, healing studies, and related psi topics, and is the author of *Telepathy, Clairvoyance and Precognition: A Re-Evaluation of some Fascinating Case Studies* (2022). A retired physiotherapy lecturer from the former Welsh College of Medicine, University of Wales, and a Fellow of the Chartered Society of Physiotherapy, he edited *Complementary Therapies for Physical Therapists* (2000), and has published chapters on the *Electrical Properties of Cells and Tissues*, the *Neurology of Skill Learning*, and the *Neurology of Pain Gating Mechanisms*. Although he has never had an ESP experience himself, he believes it is a real phenomenon and beyond reasonable doubt.

www.ingramcontent.com/pod-product-compliance
Lightning Source LLC
Chambersburg PA
CBHW032150080426
42735CB00008B/655